The
Beginning Filmmaker's
Business Guide

OTHER BOOKS BY RENÉE HARMON

How to Audition for Movies and TV
The Beginning Filmmaker's Guide to Directing

The Beginning Filmmaker's *Business Guide*

FINANCIAL, LEGAL, MARKETING, AND DISTRIBUTION BASICS OF MAKING MOVIES

Renée Harmon

Walker and Company
New York

I wish to express my gratitude to Mary Kennan Herbert,
for her adventurous spirit, which helped me to create this book,
as well as for her thoughtful guidance along the way.

Copyright © 1994 by Renée Harmon
All rights reserved. No part of this book may be reproduced or
transmitted in any form or by any means, electronic or mechanical,
including photocopying, recording, or by any information storage and
retrieval system, without permission in writing from the Publisher.

First published in the United States of America in 1994 by Walker
Publishing Company, Inc.

Published simultaneously in Canada by Thomas Allen & Son Canada,
Limited, Markham, Ontario

Library of Congress Cataloging-in-Publication Data
Harmon, Renée.
The beginning filmmaker's business guide: financial, legal, marketing, and distribution basics of
making movies / Renée Harmon.
p.   cm.
Includes bibliographical references and index.
ISBN 0-8027-1282-7. —ISBN 0-8027-7409-1 (pbk.)
1. Motion pictures—Marketing.   2. Motion pictures—Distribution—Law and legislation.
3. Motion picture industry—Finance.   4. Video recordings—Marketing.   I. Title.
PN1995.9.M29H37   1994
791.43′068—dc20   93-10977
                                                                                      CIP

The American Film Institute,
which provided the sample grant
application on pages 189–92,
is funded by the National Endowment
for the Arts.

Book design by Claire Vaccaro
Printed in the United States of America
2 4 6 8 10 9 7 5 3 1

Contents

$\mathcal{P}$reface

Never before in the motion picture business have practices and guidelines changed as much as they have during recent years. These changes have caused havoc. Many once-solid companies have ceased to exist; others, employing different business methods, have sprung up. Therefore, today more than ever, the producer, director, and/or writer must be knowledgeable about the ins and outs of getting a film off the ground.

The Beginning Filmmaker's Business Guide provides this knowledge, as it guides you through all phases important to your film's successful marketing: the movie's germinal idea (or acquisition of literary property), its sellable "hook" and distribution appeal, design of the effective, hard-hitting package (offering, prospectus), ways and means of financing your project, the nitty-gritty of today's production practices as they exist in studio deals, studio acquisition, and independent and foreign distribution as well as in the aux-iliary markets (cable, TV, and home video).

This book is a problem-identifying and problem-solving guide, giving you examples of various budget scenarios, offering/prospectus contracts, and distribution agreements that will help you give your project the professional expertise it deserves.

1.

High concept, hooks,

and

other facts of life

Have you ever asked yourself why a mediocre film is out in the theaters while a much better movie languishes in some film storage vault? The answer is that the first film is promotable, while the latter lacks the all-important advertising hooks.

A producer's knowledge about film marketing may make the difference between a movie on the screen and one on the shelves. Unless the producer has worked toward marketing from the conception of the movie's idea through the final production stages, even a thought-provoking screenplay, skilled director, exciting actors, outstanding special effects and/or stunts, as well as professional photography and editing won't get the movie into theaters. Clearly, then, you the producer ought to concern yourself with the promotable—in other words, *marketable*—elements of your film, *prior to financing.*

So let's walk through the various steps required before you can talk about finance. You accomplish this first step by keeping your mind on the audience—that is to say, your film's promotable elements that will draw the ticket-buying audience into theatres. This means you'll have to stress your movie's *high concept.*

Before going on, permit me to correct a misconception: high concept *does not* refer to:

- High budget
- Expensive star

- Well-known director
- Outstanding stunts and/or special effects
- Exotic locations

High concept applies to the fact that a commercially viable picture must provide the distributor with *promotional elements* that touch upon the audience's emotions:

- A gripping story
- Characters the audience either hates or can identify with (if these characters are to be portrayed by—at the moment—popular stars, so much the better)
- And most important, a seemingly intangible ingredient that permits the audience to let go of hidden fears, frustrations, and/or desires

Don't ever forget, "making movies" is big business. (It goes without saying that every distributor, whether major, mini-major, or independent, expects your film is of high professional quality.) But after lip service has been paid to the art and message of a film, a distributor's consideration boils down to one thing only: high concept.

Whether you have written (or intend to write) your own screenplay or are ready to spend a few hundred or many hundred thousands of dollars to option a screenplay (an area we will discuss later) or book, short story, newspaper article, or even the germ of an idea linked to any of these, always keep high concept in mind. Here are six key questions always to ask:

1. Can the basic idea be developed into a clear story line?
2. Does the basic idea feature components (hooks) that make it promotable?
3. What segment of the paying audience will the idea attract? (genre)
4. Will the idea lend itself to the creation of a catchy title?
5. Can this idea by expressed in an interesting visual way?

And since, let's admit it, there are really not any new story ideas and/or plots floating around, you may ask yourself:

6. Can this idea be turned around and/or given a new twist to give a new approach to a frequently used concept?

If none of the above can be answered in the affirmative, you know that the idea is either too vague or too complicated to be turned into a successful (read: promotable) movie. Most likely such material lacks the promotional hook, and therefore will have difficulties in finding distribution and financing.

Here are some answers to these six key questions:

1. *Clear Story Line*. Test your material's soundness and the strength of your idea by reducing it to one sentence that tells the gist of the story. Examples from fairy tales show these one-sentence truths:

Hansel and Gretel
Two children lost in the woods survive life-threatening danger.

Cinderella
Courage saves a princess and a kingdom.

Snow White
An evil queen tries to kill a beautiful girl.

Jack and the Beanstalk
A young boy outsmarts a giant.

As you take a look at the story sentence, you'll discover that each one of the old fairy tales features powerful human emotions (motives) that compel characters to do something to reach a goal based upon:

Survival
Love
Hate
Fear

The emotions "talk" to the viewer until he or she, subconsciously identifying with the character on the screen, taps into his or her own hidden emotions, fears, and/or desires.

In a nutshell, your story sentence should lead the audience to ask: Will the character accomplish his or her goal? Yet, the audience won't ask this question unless the character's goal springs from one of the above-listed emotions. These emotions in turn are the basis for the *promotional hook*.

2. *Promotional Hook.* Back to our fairy tales:

Hansel and Gretel
Hook: Children face death.

Cinderella
Hook: Love conquers all.

Snow White
Hook: Beauty is dangerous.

Jack and the Beanstalk
Hook: Intelligence outwits size.

(Just for fun, apply the above-listed hooks to some of the recently released, successful films, and you'll be surprised to see the correlation.)

Take a good look at the hooks, and you'll notice that each one of them has been designed to express loudly how scary, heartwarming, entertaining, or exciting the story is. The practice of the promotional hook goes way back to the carnival barker bellowing:

"See the bearded lady."
"See the fire eater."
"See the fearless lion tamer."

Simply imagining yourself to be a carnival barker will lead you to your story's hook and from there to its high concept.

You may train yourself in the art of recognizing high concept by taking a good, hard look at this year's five most successful movies, by studying movie ads in your local paper, or simply by perusing the *TV Guide*.

3. *Genre.* Keep a close look at genres, and decide whether your idea or script falls within any of them. In keeping with high concept, it is best to avoid mixing genres within one film. Familiarize yourself with the current selling power of each genre, but keep in mind that by the time your movie is ready for release this particular genre might be out of favor, or the market might be flooded with similar products. For this reason it is a good idea to keep a tight tab on current production schedules by reading the "trades." If you should discover a number of projects that are similar to yours, you better have some second thoughts before forging ahead.

Before beginning your project you ought to get acquainted with the distribution companies specializing in your movie's genre, and—maybe most important—familiarize yourself with the hooks promoting various genres. This information is easy to obtain through the annual new film issues of the trade papers *Variety* and *Hollywood Reporter* advertising the following film markets:

American Film Market
Los Angeles, USA (February issues)

Cannes Film Festival
Cannes, France (April issues)

MIFED
Milan, Italy (October issues)

The following is a list of basic movie genres:
Action has been, and still is, the staple of both low-budget film and multimillion-dollar blockbusters. A simple story line, based on the battle between good and evil, is mandatory. Action films sell well if presented with a different twist (familiar situations presented in different and new ways). At times when the market is flooded with action films, you'll have a tough go unless you feature a name star.

Action-Adventure usually sells well but demands exotic, or at least highly interesting, locations (e.g., the Indiana Jones trilogy).

Art Film is the most difficult genre to get financed and distributed. Such a film is hard to market. There are, however, some small distributors who, in moving a few prints from theater to theater, do an excellent job. Do not expect to make any money on your art film, yet as you exhibit it at various film festivals (not markets) and—it is hoped—garner some awards, you gain exposure for yourself and your work of cinematic art (e.g., *La Strada, Lili, Marty*).

Comedy, if the script offers hilarious situations and twists, is always a seller. Usually it does better domestically than overseas (e.g., *Some Like It Hot*).

Romantic Comedy, if featuring two well-known stars, is another marketable vehicle. Without name stars, romantic comedy is more difficult to sell (e.g., *The Graduate, Desk Set, The Quiet Man, High Society,* all the Spencer Tracy–Katharine Hepburn films).

Docudrama features a story based upon a nonfictional frightening, unusual, or controversial event. Theatrically and in home video this genre has proven to be less successful, but is always needed for cable and network TV (e.g., *All the President's Men, Paths of Glory, The Right Stuff*).

Mystery. The traditional mystery has by now been firmly entrenched in TV programming, and is therefore less prevalent on the big screen (e.g., *The Third Man, Dr. Crippen on Board, Murder on the Orient Express*).

Horror is an old standby that never fails to attract viewers. Blockbusters of course depend on extraordinary—and expensive—special effects. But even a low-budget film will find buyers if based on an interesting premise (e.g., *The Creature from the Black Lagoon, Frankenstein*).

Psychological Thriller. The psychological thriller has replaced the traditional murder mystery on the big screen. If your psychological thriller has believable characters and an extraordinary hook, then go for it (e.g., *Fatal Attraction*).

4. *Title*. It is a must to carry the high concept over to a film's title; a film's title presents the audience with the hook about its content.

As you think about the best title for your movie, ask yourself:

What does the title mean and/or what message does the title communicate?

What emotion does the title evoke?

The working titles of many of my films were changed by the distributor for catchier ones. Here are a few examples:

Revenge	to	*Lady Streetfighter*
Chill Factor	to	*Frozen Scream*
Bikers	to	*Hellriders*
The Idol	to	*Jungle Trap*

Granted, all the above titles were chosen for low-budget films, but the principle applies to multimillion-dollar productions as well.

5. *Visual Interpretation of Ideas*. Beware of any ideas that depend upon the verbal expression of goals and/or emotions primarily. Always keep in mind that film is a visual medium that fosters visual expression. (Most stage plays that were adapted to the screen turned out to be photographed renderings of the play, and therefore failed to grab the movie audience's empathy.) This does not imply, however, that a film depends upon the director's expertise in creating unique camera setups and moves. Fact is, many a film failed to

grip the audience's response (and therefore failed at the box office) because its cinematography did draw too much attention from the movie's pictorial aspects, instead of focusing on the director's responsibility *to tell a gripping story.*

6. *Twists in Concepts and Ideas.* Let's face it, writers of novels and screenplays have only a limited number of basic plots at their disposal. Even magazine stories and news reports seem to repeat the same incidents over and over again. Then why do we read books, go to the movies, and watch TV? We do, because the old and familiar has been changed in such a way as to make it new and exciting.

Take another look at the previously discussed fairy tales and you will discover that a host of movies has developed from their basic—and very simple—concepts. Here are but a few examples, randomly selected:

Jack and the Beanstalk
A young boy outsmarts a powerful giant.

Burning Bed
A woman escapes from her abusive husband.

Cinderella
Prince Charming saves Cinderella from her mean stepmother and ugly stepsisters.

Pretty Woman
A girl who makes her living as a prostitute meets the man who "saves" her.

Hansel and Gretel
The witch lures children into her gingerbread house.

Silence of the Lambs
A psychopath imprisons young girls and kills them.

Snow White
The queen tries to kill her rival—the beautiful Snow White.

Dressed to Kill
A cross-dresser stalks attractive women.

Therefore, if you find a story or idea that seems suitable, if a little trite, try to turn it upside down, adjust it, change it, create new characters, and you'll be surprised about the unique concept you'll come up with.

Advertising

As the producer, you will eventually have to pay for the release prints (about $1,500 for each 35mm print). Contrary to common belief, the distributor *does* *not* pay for the prints. The distribution company only *advances* the required sum, and—never forget this—is first in line for recoupment. Moreover, most distributors attempt to put some of the advertising expenses upon the producer's shoulders.*

The following are the traditional advertising tools employed:

Trailers for theatrical promotion (teasers)
Trailers for TV promotion (spots)
Radio blurbs
One-sheets (posters)
Mats for newspaper advertising
Sell sheets
Box cover for home video release
Screening in foreign film markets

If you, the producer, are able to pay at least partially for the prints at the movie's release, you'll have a strong negotiation point as far as advertising is concerned.

Trailers. Here we are speaking about two kinds of trailers: the "teasers" customarily shown in theaters and the spots shown on TV. While the cost of a teaser is negligible, since it involves only some expenses for editing and printing, TV spots—especially if shown in prime time and in major cities—may run into millions. (Needless to say, a low-budget film does not require any TV spots.) TV spots are also important for a film's home video sales; wholesalers tend to hinge the size of their order upon the scope of the motion picture distributor's TV advertising.

Radio blurbs. Radio blurbs are an excellent and not exorbitantly costly advertising tool, if your film has either a strong musical score or catchy, unusual auditory moments.

One-sheets (posters). The advertising tool demanding close attention is the one-sheet (poster), not as much for its value as a lobby display as for the fact that all graphic advertising (sell sheets, newspaper mats, and home video box covers) is based upon the eye-catching and emotional-reponse-demanding one-sheet. My advice is that you begin working on the concept of your one-sheet as early as your film's preproduction time. Many producers even have

---

*The producer's participation in advertising expenses will be discussed in the chapter on distribution.

their one-sheet's concept ready for their offering and/or prospectus. Some producers, getting ready to offer their films at the film markets, even create one-sheets for films that neither are in preproduction nor have acquired funding.

Here are some pointers about your one-sheet key art:

- Keep the concept strong but simple.
- Do not include too many details. Keep in mind that your key art has to work in reduced formats. Even a very small newspaper ad has to convey the film's hook.
- Remember that your full-color one-sheet will be printed in black-and-white for newspaper advertising.

Title treatment is equally important, and as with your graphic art it must reduce well. The one-sheet shows two title elements: the copy line and the tag line. The copy line is placed *above* the film's title. It sets up what the film is all about. It has to grab the viewer's attention and emotional response immediately. For this very reason the copy line is imperative for the low-budget film. Here are a few examples:

COPY LINE: They came out of the grave . . .
TITLE: *Scalps*
COPY LINE: Beware rapists, killers, and muggers . . .
TITLE: *The Executioner*
COPY LINE: The dream you cannot escape . . .
TITLE: *Nightmare*

If these copy lines seem a bit too colorful—read "cheap"— don't worry, major studios use similar scintillating "orations" to sell their product. (Your art film, of course, demands a more subdued way of advertising.)

The tag line appears *after* the title and acknowledgments:

TITLE: *Scalps*
TAG LINE: . . . to get revenge.
TITLE: *The Executioner*
TAG LINE: . . . is back to get you.
COPY LINE: *Nightmare*
TAG LINE: . . . you haven't got a chance.

Once your film ad receives favorable reviews, add those blurbs to your tag line.

Shop around for your artwork. It is not unusual to spend several hundred thousand dollars (or more), but there is no doubt that you can obtain highly satisfactory artwork for about $5,000. All you have to do is shop around.

Here are a few suggestions:

Contact local art schools or the fine arts department of a university or college. You may put an inquiry on their bulletin board or enlist the assistance of one of the instructors.

A small ad in the "wanted" column of local newspapers should get you in contact with free-lance artists.

If you have some contact with one of the big studios, you may be able to find out whether someone on their staff might be willing to moonlight for you.

All students, and some free-lance artists, will gladly accept a lower fee in exchange for printed samples for his or her portfolio.

Presently distribution companies prefer illustrations for their key art. These illustrations are derived from either sketches or photos.

Once the artwork has been completed to your and the distributor's satisfaction, an offset printer will do the color separations, add the copy, and do the actual printing.

Sell sheets. Sell sheets are used as "throwaways" at film markets and are given to home video retailers. They advertise either a specific film or a number of films. Sell sheets will be printed both in color and in black-and-white.

Mats. This term derives from the old "hot type" era, and refers to your film's ads for newspapers and sell sheets. You need mats in several sizes to fit various printing requirements and ad spaces.

Home video box cover. Your home video distributors either supply the wholesaler with sleeves to be inserted into the plastic envelope covering the box or have cardboard boxes printed.

Except for blockbuster movies, it is packaging that makes a modestly viable theatrical film into a hot one for home video. The cover is the key element of the home video release. With your home video sale in mind, and knowing that your one-sheets will adorn the home video box, you should choose a strong color scheme. Don't ever try to save money by deciding upon a black-and-white box cover; no one will look at your film, much less rent or buy it. A *three-color* job is a must for your one-sheets. Still, you can save a bundle of money and give your one-sheets the desired three-color effect by choosing colored stock on which you print *two-color* key art. For my film *Night of Terror* we used black stock and had the artwork printed in red and silver.

Publicity

Publicity, if thoughtfully orchestrated and combined with effective advertising (P&A), can be immensely helpful. Needless to say, the publicity campaign *should not* be employed in lieu of advertising.

Publicity consists of your film's free exposure via magazine and newspaper articles, TV talk shows, and news shows. You'll need a press kit and electronic press kit and, most important, a public relations (PR) firm to handle your publicity. Granted, a PR firm, if well connected and established, is expensive. True, there are many PR firms around, but only one with clout will do you and your film any good. Don't be taken in by sweet words and flashy pamphlets. Before you hire a PR firm, interview several firms, *ask for client lists* (including telephone numbers), and call these clients. In addition, take a look at magazines and newspapers featuring articles or pictures about the firm's clients. Make certain the firm's sample press releases are recent. Question every PR firm long and hard. Find out whether the firm is familiar with PR techniques pertaining to motion pictures, and if it has excellent media connections.

The effective PR firm *must* have nationwide contacts. After all, you want to read about your movie in national magazines, and you want to see your stars on network or syndicated TV.

Obviously, all publicity concentrates on your stars and—if well known—your director. Don't expect, however, that you, the producer, will be part of the "hype." Accept the fact that you, the person who has nurtured the project through all the travails of rewrite, financing, casting, and so on, are not appropriate fodder for the media.

Don't hesitate to negotiate the PR firm's fee. All PR firms demand retainer fees. You'll have to apply a (hefty) monthly fee regardless of whether any promotion results from the firm's effort. And this is the catch: You'll pay for their efforts and not the results.

It is obvious that, for a small art film seeing territorial distribution only (we will discuss distribution patterns later on) and being exhibited in a few selected theaters, an expensive nationwide PR campaign is a waste of time and money. For your art film you'll do best to hire territorial PR firms and have your film given some exposure in national magazines catering to the audience interested in art films only.

It is a must to get in touch with PR firms as soon as possible, and it is a good idea to have at least *some* publicity material ready before you contact any of them. A long "lead-in" period is mandatory. Magazines have to be approached about three months (if not longer) prior to the publicity target date. Therefore, if your film has been scheduled for a summer release, your PR firm *must* contact magazines no later than March.

Should a magazine insist upon screening your movie, make arrangements to do so about five to six months before your movie's release date. But here's a word of warning: Do not get suckered into showing a rough cut of your as yet uncompleted film.* Since magazine editors are not accomplished filmmakers, your film, at best, won't be reviewed; at worst it might be set up for poisonous barbs.

Once you have decided on a PR firm, provide them with all the photos, dates, and written material they require. They will need these materials to put together a press kit and an electronic press kit.

Press kit. Think about publicity while your film is in production. You will need a still photographer to shoot "stills" throughout the production. (You'll need plenty of stills anyway for your foreign market, where lobby displays of stills are very much in vogue.)

Electronic press kit. An electronic press kit may be as short as five to seven minutes, or it may stretch into a full thirty-minute documentary. Domestically only short versions of a press kit are asked for, while a number of overseas TV stations (Germany, Italy, France, Spain) gratefully accept (free of charge) your documentary. The electronic press kit is a combination of "behind-the-scenes shots" of the filming of your movie, some actual film clips, and interviews with the stars. The behind-the-scenes segments are easy to do. Here are a few suggestions:

* Actors: Actors in makeup session
Actors and crew at lunch
Actors rehearsing

*A "rough cut" refers to a film that is incomplete as far as final editing, music, and sound effects are concerned.

* Director: Conferring with script supervisor
            Setting up a shot
* Stunts: Preparation for a stunt
            Rigging of stunt vehicles

And don't forget the "in-depth interview" with your stars. By the way, have you ever wondered why a world-renowned movie star granted your local station's anchorperson an interview? Well, here is the answer: While shooting your movie, you'll tape your star's answers to questions that appear character generated (printed) on a tape between the answers. Your local station edits their anchorperson in, and presto you'll have a "personalized" interview.

It's as easy as that, and it looks great.

My advice is that you have about a thousand electronic press kits ready at your PR firm. Editing and duplicating a press kit on tape is inexpensive.

Screenings. All major studios and a great number of independent distributors test the market via prerelease screenings.

Testing the market consists of specific tests in three or four different TV spots and in a number of newspaper ads featuring different artwork, titles, copy lines, and tag lines. The film is previewed in a variety of areas on the East and West coasts, in the Midwest, and in the South, as well as in various theaters located in different socioeconomic areas. According to the audience's response, the film will be targeted (advertised) to a certain socioeconomic group and therefore will be more heavily promoted and exhibited in certain areas, while not shown in others.

Audiences respond to the film via questionnaires. The following questions are those most likely to be asked. Respondents rate their answers on a scale of 1 (highest) to 4 (lowest).

Your favorite scenes
    action scenes _____
    love scenes _____
    scenes between Lydia and James _____
    others _____
Your least-liked scenes
    boxing scenes _____
    love scenes _____
    family reunion scenes _____
    others _____

Your favorite character
    Lydia _____
    James _____
    Bill _____
    Rita _____
What did you like best in the movie? _____
What did you like least in the movie? _____
Would you recommend the movie to your friends? _____
Total overall rating:
    Excellent _____
    Very good _____
    Good _____
    Poor _____

Considering the questionnaire's results the distributor may increase or decrease the film's advertising budget and change the ad campaign. For instance, if the film had been targeted as an action film but the questionnaire revealed the love scenes as audience favorites, the film's one-sheet (artwork and copy) will be changed accordingly.

If the film tested poorly with affluent audiences, it will be targeted (posters, TV spots, radio blurbs) to a more middle-class audience. If the film tested poorly in rural areas but did fairly well in urban areas, the distribution pattern will follow course.

Prerelease screenings, a.k.a. sneak previews, are expensive, at times helpful, but most often confusing. The result of a sneak preview may compel the producer to change the film via reediting or (worse) reshooting. As a result, there is always the chance that such a "reworked" film may lose the story's basic direction and possibly the film's theme as well.

Granted, market research serves its purpose, but I'm afraid it is a far less powerful device than most distribution executives claim. Who knows whether the questionnaires have been filled in thoughtfully and specifically? Many people don't care. Some put marks wherever their pencil happens to land. Some resent having to fill in these "darned" cards; they come to the movies to be entertained, not to be part of a survey. Others enjoy the opportunity to "cut those Hollywood characters down to size." Comparatively few viewers take the time to answer thoughtfully.

And there are producers who participate in the not-uncommon practice of bringing suitcases full of filled-in cards to their screenings, all—naturally—waxing enthusiastic about the movie.

In my opinion it is a toss-up whether a considerable amount of money (and time) ought to be spent on sneaks. While changing promotional and distribution patterns has some validity, I doubt the merit of any last-minute reediting or reshooting. If you have targeted your film wisely from its conception on and are working with a distributor experienced in your film's genre, you may as well forgo market research.

Promotion for the Special Elements of Movies Made for Home Video

Admittedly, the extensive promotional pattern discussed in this section does not apply for the low-budget film that has been produced for the home video market, one that sees a token domestic theatrical release only.

Let's not kid ourselves. A made-for-home-video movie can in no way compete with any major film that, because of its theatrical exposure, has enjoyed extensive promotion. This in no way indicates that the made-for-home-video film is in any way inferior to its major-studio counterpart. The fact remains, however, that it did not enjoy the latter's promotional advantage, and therefore, at least in the retailer's mind, is second-rate.

You, the producer, have to supply the distribution company with almost life-size standup "cutouts" of your star (or the movie's main promotable element), participate in advertising your film in the appropriate home video magazines, and last but not least, supply the key art and copy for an eye-catching box cover.

In short, you'll have to spend your advertising dollars wisely.

2.

The package:

how to put together

your offering/prospectus

Your chances of attracting a studio deal, independent distributor, and investors hinge on a complete and effective presentation of your *offering/prospectus*—in short, the package. (You will approach investors with an offering, and studios with a prospectus.) You have to convince investors, studio and distribution executives alike, that you, the producer, are able to helm the project. If you are a novice, you of course have to work harder than your more experienced counterparts. Your offering/prospectus must look and sound professional, that is to say, impressive but not flashy. You achieve this by creating a complete and convincing combination of artistic and promotable elements that provide a picture of the film's favorable economic prospects.

You should also at this point (if you are not pursuing a studio deal) obtain competent legal advice. Financing a movie (or any other venture) is fraught with problems, and I cannot emphasize strongly enough the importance of having an expert entertainment attorney on your team. All materials of your offering and all documents you may attach should be approved by your attorney.

The four key elements of your package are

1. The film's creative elements (artistic merit):
   Screenplay
   Stars

Director

Locations

2. The film's promotable elements:

Star

Genre

Hook

3. The film's positive financial elements:

The producer's expertise (track record, showing that producer has brought in previous films on time and on budget)

The film's viable financial structure (budget)

4. The film's sales potential (a letter of intent from a reliable distribution company) if you are trying to interest investors

After reading the above list, you'll realize that you have to give your prospective investors not only a strong economic incentive but also the confidence that the project is viable, that is to say that others, all experts in their fields, are interested in participating. You'll have an excellent chance of getting your project off the ground if you have letters of intent from a reliable distribution company, known directors, and a recognizable star.

In regard to the above elements, you are facing a Catch-22 dilemma. Many stars, directors, and distributors refuse to commit themselves unless the project has been financed. On the other hand, investors are reluctant to "sign on the dotted line" unless the above elements are attached to the project. The only way to overcome this seemingly insurmountable hurdle is to ask your prospective investors for a letter of interest. Such a letter does not represent a commitment on anyone's part, but does confirm an enthusiasm for the project.

In case you have entrusted an agent with the task of interesting a director and stars in your project and this agent works for an agency known to package* films, you may face the danger that the packaging agency contacts *your* investors, firms the deal, and leaves you out in the cold. You should protect yourself against such practice by having your attorney draw up agreements, binding your prospective investors to deal only with you and your attorney on "said" project (your film).

On the other hand, if you do not look for financing, but are pursuing a

---

*"Packagers" are agencies providing a project with the necessary elements: stars, writer, director, who are under contract with the agency. The agency submits the project to major studios.

studio deal,* it is best not to contact any stars or a director, but to wait for the studio's suggestions.

And now, let's discuss your package in detail.

How your offering/prospectus (package) should look.

Your offering/prospectus must have a professional appearance:

- Have a competent typist type your presentation.
- Choose a plastic spiral-bound folder.
- Use heavy paper stock for your cover.
- *Do not* stamp the front cover with a "confidential" stamp (there is nothing confidential about your project); such labels smack of amateurism.
- *Do not* include photographs of stars or locations (again, this gives your presentation an amateurish look).
- *Do not* clutter your presentation with graphic designs (these make your presentation difficult to peruse).

Now that your package looks professional, let's discuss what should be included in it. The following is a list of the main elements:

Cover Page
The Offering
Legal Entities
Story Synopsis
Script and Story Outline
Stars and Director (Letters of Interest)
Producer
Key Personnel
Distribution Agreement (Letter of Interest)
Project Status
Financing
   Budget
   Risk-Return
   Fiscal Control
   Investor's Protection
   Overall
   Share of Profits

*A major studio finances and distributes your film.

Marketing
   Promotable Elements
   Advertising and Publicity
   Viability
   Suggested Distribution Plan

Cover page:
   Title of your film
   Project description: A motion picture project
   Brochure description: A financing outline
   Name of production company and logo
   Name of producer
   Date

The offering. This is a statement of what you are offering prospective investors: "Offering [amount of monies to be raised] in limited partnership, corporation, or joint venture interests in [name of production company] to finance the motion picture [title of your movie]."

It is very important that (after discussing the matter with your attorney) you add the following qualifying clause: "These securities [partnerships] are offered pursuant to an exemption from registration with the United States Securities and Exchange Commission. The Commission does not pass upon the merits of any securities [partnership shares], nor does it pass upon the accuracy or completeness of any offering or other selling literature."

Legal entities. This segment shows the legal form of your venture. Again, in establishing the decided upon legal entity, your attorney's advice is urgently needed. The basic options are as follows:

- *Limited partnership.* The investors become Limited Partners, whereas the producer remains the General Partner. The Limited Partners are protected from any liability in excess of their investment. The General Partner does not enjoy this protection.

- *Corporation.* The investors acquire *nontransferable* shares of stock in the production company.

- *Investment contract.* The producer and/or the production company contracts with the investors re interest rate (not profits) to be received from the invested monies.

• *Joint venture/general partnership.* A few partners share risk and profit with the producer.

The merits and pitfalls of each venture will be discussed in detail later. Since financing is such a wide and, let's admit, complicated field, an entire chapter will be devoted to it. (See chapter 8.)

Story synopsis. Make certain that the synopsis contains all marketable/promotional aspects of the prospective film. For this purpose I like to submit a teaser and the story outline. The teaser, very much like the one used on a home-video box cover, highlights the film's promotional aspects. The following teaser was used in the offering for my horror film *Frozen Scream.*

> Two misdirected scientists think they have discovered a technique for achieving immortality: lowering body temperatures to slow down the aging process. But this technique has one fatal flaw—a mind- and soul-altering effect that turns the patients into frozen zombies.
>
> When Ann discovers her husband's poisoned body, she goes into shock and is hospitalized. The doctors try to convince her that Tom, her husband, died of a heart attack, but her nightmarish visions lead her to believe otherwise. Her curiosity takes her to the doctors' secret laboratory where she discovers a freezer full of frozen zombies—including Tom.
>
> Ann escapes the zombies' violent attack, but others are not as fortunate. Soon the zombies are everywhere, attacking and "recruiting" new victims for the mad doctors' experiments.

Keep the story's details for the story outline. And be aware that unless you are offering an art film, or asking for a grant, you should not go into your film's theme, that is to say, your concerns about esoteric issues that are important to you. Remember, the partners you are soliciting will join you in your venture for one reason only: They want to make some profit. Films that deal with issues don't have "legs" (don't sell well).

Script and story outline. Include the completed script as well as a detailed story outline in your package.

Stars and director. We already discussed the dilemma faced in trying to obtain the precious letters of intent. But in lieu of those you should at least try to obtain letters of interest. Although these letters aren't a commitment to anything, they look good in your offering.

Unfortunately, for the beginning producer it is not easy to get the cooperation of recognizable actors and actresses. This difficulty is compounded by the fact that the first-time producer most likely has no development funds earmarked to pay options to a prospective star.

Over and over I've heard stories about scripts delivered to stars and agents that were never read; about telephone calls that were never returned. Let's assume these eager-beaver producers went about their business the wrong way. They sent their scripts to actors who, commanding "honoraria" of four to five million dollars, were far beyond the producer's status in this industry. Or they sent their scripts to one of the big agencies, such as William Morris, CAA, ICM. Now don't get me wrong, if you submit a terrific script to be packaged by the respective agency, as a first-time producer you have at least a fighting chance to be invited for an initial interview. (It goes without saying that your script *must* have been written by a recognizable writer and *must* qualify for the standard budget of between ten and twenty million dollars.) But no major agency will consider any low-budget not-yet-funded script if asked to interest one of their stars in the project.

So what is the first-time producer going to do? After all, a recognizable star is the key element in any offering. There are a few simple steps that should result in recognizable names providing letters of interest. First discuss your project with some medium-sized distributors. If you do not find willing ears, contact a reliable "distributor for hire."* Show your script and show your budget. (In case you do not live close to a metropolis, consult the respective film market issues of *Variety* and *Hollywood Reporter* for names and addresses. You can gauge a distributor's importance by the size of their ads.) Try to get the distributor's letter of interest. Even if you should fail to do so, ask the distributor to suggest a few names, people he/she thinks are right for your project, that is to say, are recognizable. This in turn means these names may not be recognizable by the public at large, but are known to the industry domestically and overseas. But be well aware that the *recognizability* of any name hinges upon the size of your budget. For a budget ranging in the vicinity of one and a half million, you will attract a "better" name (not necessarily a better actor) than for a budget of $750,000. After you have collected a few names, call your local SAG office and ask for the actor's agent's name and address. Don't send your script out cold. Call the agent first, tell him/her that you have a terrific script with an excellent part for his or her client, and that the distribution company has not only shown interest in your script, but also

*More about the "distributor for hire" in chapter 5.

has suggested the agent's client for the lead. Then submit your script and your budget, and watch the ball roll.

Producer. Do have an experienced producer on board as one of the key elements of your package? He or she has to have a track record—has to be known to bring in a film on budget and on time.

My advice is that for your first project you hire a skilled producer, and content yourself (if you are instrumental in obtaining financing) with the title of executive producer.

And now, please hold your horses and don't throw this book aside. The following advice comes straight from my heart: If you, the producer, also are the screenwriter with as yet no directing notches on your belt (regardless of whether you attended directing courses), please do not insist that you and only you can direct the film. Many otherwise promising projects have run aground on the treacherous rocks of a writer-producer-director's contention "Only I will provide the film with the artistic and creative elements it deserves. Only I ought to direct the film." True, you probably know your script and your movie's theme better than any other person in this world, but remember, investors invest in a movie for one purpose only, to make money. You, the novice director-producer, by polishing your brainchild's minute details, may be tempted to go over time and budget. The experienced director, on the other hand, though as excited about the project as you are, views a film objectively, maintaining necessary emotional distance.

And even the experienced director needs an equally experienced producer, one who adheres to these principles:

- Choose a well-constructed script, featuring a clear plot line that is based on honest human emotions.
- See to it that the film is competently acted, directed, and photographed.
- Always be aware of the film's promotional hook.
- And last but not least, remember Billy Wilder's famous advice: "Thou shall not bore."

Key personnel. It is absolutely essential that your offering/prospectus name certain key people as part of your team. These include a production manager, a production accountant, an art director, and a cinematographer.

If the project at hand is your first attempt at producing, you ought to contact a *production manager* (PM) who has a mile-long credit list. Quite naturally, the financing sources assume that in case you encounter difficulties, the PM will jump into the breach. The PM is the liaison between the producer and the "shoot." He or she hires crew and equipment, searches in concert with the director and art director for locations, and is responsible for the sufficient delivery of raw stock for each day's shooting. One of the PM's most difficult tasks is to keep the production running, that is to say, to make certain that each scheduled setup has been shot and that the production does not run into "golden time." If you remember that crew and cast will not only receive overtime pay but also "meal penalties" (for meals not provided for overtime work), you will agree that staying on time is mandatory. Also, if for any reason any scheduled setups have to be carried over to the next day, the following problems may arise: The shooting schedule may have to be revised; the location needed may not be available for another day; or one of the actors may be unavailable.

You will agree, the PM's job is not an easy one. Frictions occur between the director and PM, as the director insists on "one more take" (which stretches into five takes), the cinematographer opts for a more elaborate light plot, and the star demands more close-ups.

Since it is *your* job to keep the show running smoothly—that is to say, to keep each situation from exploding—the PM will ask you to make the final decisions. It is exactly for this reason that you must have either solid producing experience or have hired a well-qualified PM.

Traditionally the PM writes the budget and breaks down the script into a realistic shooting schedule. I advise strongly that the producer does this job first, then with the PM finalizes the budget, and, adding the input of the PM, director, and cinematographer, goes over the breakdown again. It is during the preproduction period that disagreements can be settled most easily, and areas where frictions may arise can be anticipated and may be dealt with.

Many investors insist that they hire the *production accountant*. He or she is the production's watchdog, who turns in daily and weekly production accounts. Insist that the production accountant is present on the set, takes care of the miscellaneous items to be paid out of petty cash, and pays the bills for rentals, crew salaries, permits, and minor daily locations. The weekly accountings will include payments for cast, locations, lab fees, and raw stock, and later on sound lab and editing expenses. The production accountant is a blessing in disguise, as he or she keeps the PM from dealing with minor monetary matters. The daily expense account keeps the producer abreast of expenditures (seemingly minor ones may turn into an avalanche), while the weekly reports do point out any area where the production is in danger of going overboard. It is important that copies of both daily and weekly reports be sent to each investor.

Technically neither the *cinematographer* nor the *art director* is a key person on a project, yet it is wise to list their expertise in the offering/prospectus. Both have to be experts in their respective fields. It is the art director who gives a film its look and atmosphere. Take a good look at the art director's portfolio:

- Do sets/locations express the film's mood?
- Do sets/locations fit the film's theme?
- Are sets/locations unique or run-of-the-mill?

Discuss your budget requirements with the art director and see whether he or she can meet your time and budget demands. And always remember, it is the art director who, with the director and cinematographer, brings the script's idea and theme to life.

It is the cinematographer who has not only to bring in a visually acceptable film but also who, in many instances—because of slow setups and overly complicated light plots—may contribute to a film's going overtime and consequently going over budget. Before looking at any cinematographer's demo reel,* get names and addresses, as well as telephone numbers, of his or her previous employers. Contact these producers, and ask about the cinematographer's

- Work habits
- Attitude
- How he/she got along with others—the crew, director, and producer
- Setup times (fast or slow)
- Light plots (effective or ineffective). Additional requirements that are costly, such as scaffold lighting or excessive use of tracks for camera movements

As you look at the cinematographer's "demo reel" do not be taken in by the beautiful vision you see on the screen. Ask your director to check out:

---

*A demo reel is a tape that shows excerpts of the cinematographer's previous work.

- How is a scene lit? Does lighting help to set the mood and
  atmosphere of the scene?
- Are actors lit attractively?
- Transitions. As the film moves from scene to scene, is the lighting
  appropriate? Is there a smooth change in color values?
- Framing of shots. Will they adapt to later TV conversion?
- Are camera moves executed professionally?

Get together with the director and cinematographer, discuss your film, find out whether they see the film in the same way you do. Probe whether the cinematographer will go along with your ideas and will support these with creative suggestions of his/her own.

Distribution agreement. To negotiate a binding distribution agreement is unusual, unless you are a successful producer known to produce films that "have legs" (sell well). And don't forget, a distribution agreement is only worth the paper it is written on, even if the distribution company (regardless of size) is known as a reliable one. A distribution agreement issued by a fly-by-night company will do your project more harm than good. As previously mentioned, most distributing companies are more than reluctant to furnish you with a letter of intent unless you have your financing in place, and the best you can expect is the letter of interest. But don't let this deter you. Simply point out the unshakable truth—that a more favorable distribution agreement can be obtained once the film has been completed and a release print can be shown.

Project Status (Time line)

Twelve weeks—preproduction (before shooting commences)
  Polishing the script in concert with the director
  Location scouting
  Studio rental
  Conferences with key personnel (art director,
    cinematographer, stunt coordinator, special effects lab and
    person)
  Crew assembly
  Interviews with editor, production manager, musical director
  Discussion with agents regarding stars
  Final preparation of budget

Location breakdown and final shooting script
Hiring of key personnel
Callbacks of secondary actors
Conferences with postproduction facilities (lab, sound lab, editing)
Four weeks (before shooting commences)
Final casting of actors
Rehearsal of actors
Contracts with editor, labs, editing facilities, musical director
Contracts with production and postproduction facilities
Wardrobe designs and fittings
Contract locations and/or studio
Commence building sets (if applicable)
Set insurance, completion bond (if necessary), obtain city and/or county permits
Six weeks
Principal photography
Begin preediting dailies
Eight weeks (postproduction editing phase)
Edit film
Edit sound (dialog and sound effects)
Edit music
Six weeks (postproduction—final phase)
Mix and foley
SD/FX
Negative cutting
Opticals
Optical soundtrack
Titles
Timing of answer print
Answer print

Financing. It is important that you submit as detailed a budget as possible. The following is the budget for the motion picture project *High Treason** (International Film Partnerships) for a motion picture budget for $2.5 million. This budget serves as an example only—every film has to be budgeted differently.

*By permission of International Film Partnerships, Michael R. Gardina, general partner.

Maybe you'll have to spend more on locations, the star, special effects, or stunts—it all depends on your film.

The term "above-line cost" refers to the money paid for story and rights, producer's unit, direction, cast, agent's fee, and above-the-line fringe benefits, while "below the line" refers to the cost of actually shooting the film, including such diverse items as lab cost, locations, crew salaries, equipment rental, cost for editing, and music. These items include a 10 percent contingency fee, covering legal expenses, finder's fee, and so on.

The total sum of these below-the-line expenditures are called the *bottom line*.

The sum total of above- and below-the-line costs (including the completely finished and acceptable release print and at least some advertising material such as trailers, radio blurbs, and newspaper mats, and one sheets) is called the *negative cost* of a film.

Traditionally, the above-line cost of a film should be one-third the below-the-line cost, two-thirds of the negative cost. That is to say, if a film has been budgeted for $2,500,000, then the above-line cost should not be more than $833,000. In today's market, however, where even minor stars (deserving or not) demand fees of $1,000,000, and where well-known names, especially for home video and foreign sales, are mandatory, the picture has changed. Still, do not let the production values of your film suffer; it is not the dollar amount that shows on the screen, but the producer's and everyone's expertise.

Here are some suggestions:

- Consolidate locations. If you have scheduled the Smiths' living room at location A, and the Millers' living room at location B, consolidate by shooting both at location A. A clever art director can give a room many different looks.
- Consolidate light plots. Discuss all light plots at length with your cinematographer. Work out a general light plot that covers an entire area, and change lights as required to shoot specific areas.
- Change night shots to "day-for-night" shots. Night shots are expensive to set up and to light. By attaching specific filters to a camera's lens, one can change daylight to night. It helps, of course, if one is blessed with bright sunlight. The sunshine translates to eerie "moonshine."
- Move quickly from one set to the next by having your art director's

crew "dress" (set up props, furniture, draperies, and so on); have the light crew light set #2, while you shoot on set #1.

- If you have many exterior locations scheduled, always—being observant of poor weather conditions—schedule interior shots as a stopgap measure.
- Make sure your actors are well rehearsed.
- Hire only actors who have on-camera experience.
- Watch out for temperamental actors. Find out whether or not an actor/actress follows the director's suggestions willingly and easily. Replace an ego-centered actor with another, better-adjusted, one.
- Investigate whether expensive special effects can be made more palatable price-wise, by building miniatures. This advice holds especially true if you work with explosions or burning buildings.
- If you have only on-set rehearsals, have your director rehearse actors while lights are being changed. (Light changes take long; he/she will have plenty of rehearsal time.)
- Avoid time-consuming shots, of planes landing, busy city streets, shorelines, gambling places, nightclubs, party scenes, church interiors and exteriors. Buy "stock shots" instead. These are unused outtakes other production companies have sold to labs. You'll find addresses of these firms either in a production Blue Book (any bookstore specializing in theatrical and film books carries it) or by inquiring with a lab.
- And most important: Do not cut your preproduction time short. Preproduction is the key to a film's being brought in on time and within budget.

BUDGET

1100	Story and Rights	
	01. Screenplay	$25,000
	02. Idea for screenplay	5,000
	03. Printing	500
	Subtotal:	$30,500

1200	Producer's Unit	
	01. Executive producer	$ 75,000
	02. Producer	75,000

03. Associate producer		7,000
08. Legal and auditing		25,000
	Subtotal:	$182,000

1300 Direction

01. Director		$50,000
02. Assistant director		8,000
	Subtotal:	$58,000

1400 Cast

01. STAR: (either alternate I or alternate II)

Alternate I:		
Star A		$1,000,000
Alternate II:		
Star A		500,000
Star B		500,000
02. Supporting		
Costar		50,000
2 or 3 supporting stars		20,400
3-day players		3,600
15, 1-day players		6,300
	Subtotal:	$1,080,300

1500 Agent's Fees

01. 10% Star's Salary		$100,000
02. 10% Actor's agents		8,030
	Subtotal:	$108,030

1900 Above-the-line Fringe Benefits

01. Writer's WGA pension, H&W (12.5%)		$ 3,125
02. Producer's units		-0-
03. Director (non-DGA)		-0-
04. Cast SAG pension, H&W (12.5%)		10,037
Star SAG pension, H&W (12%)		125,000
	Subtotal:	$138,162

2000 Production Staff

01. Manager		$10,000
02. Script supervisor		6,000
08. Production accountant		3,000
	Subtotal:	$19,000

2200	Set Design		
	01. Art director		$ 9,000
	02. Assistant Art Director		3,200
	03. Purchasers		5,000
	04. Rentals		3,000
	05. Damages		1,000
		Subtotal:	$21,200

2300	Set Construction		
	01. Construction		$ 2,000
		Subtotal:	$ 2,000

2500	Set Operation		
	01. Key grip		$ 3,600
	02. Second grip		3,000
	03. Slate		3,000
	04. 3 Grip assistants		5,400
	05. 2 Production assistants		1,200
	06. Equipment rental		4,200
	07. Damages and losses		1,000
	08. Purchases		500
		Subtotal:	$21,900

2600	Special Effects		
	Generator rental		300
	Oil and gas		50
	Fogger		300
	Liquid fog		100
	Gun rental		200
		Subtotal:	$950

2700	Set Dressing		
	14. Purchases		500
	15. Rentals		500
	16. Damages		200
		Subtotal:	$1,200

2800	Petty Cash		
	16. Petty cash		$1,200
		Subtotal:	$1,200

2900	Wardrobe		
	Purchases		$5,000
	Cleaning		300
	Wardrobe girl		1,800
		Subtotal:	$7,100
3100	Makeup and Hair Dressing		
	01. Key makeup person		$3,000
	02. 2 Assistants		3,600
	03. Purchases		1,000
	04. Special effects makeup		200
		Subtotal:	$7,800
3200	Lighting		
	01. Gaffer		$ 6,000
	02. Best boy		3,000
	03. Assistant		2,400
	11. Burnouts, carbons, gels		2,000
	12. Purchases		1,500
	17. Rental		12,800
	18. Repairs		500
		Subtotal:	$28,200
3300	Production Sound		
	01. Mixer		$ 6,000
	02. Boom man		3,000
	03. Tape		300
	06. Equipment rental		8,000
		Subtotal:	$17,300
3400	Camera		
	01. Director of photography		$12,000
	02. Camera operator		6,000
	03. Focus assistant		4,800
	04. Loader		3,000
	05. Still man		2,400
	16. Purchases		2,700
	17. Camera maintenance		300
	19. Loss and damages		1,000
	20. Camera package rental		26,000
		Subtotal:	$58,200

3500	Transportation		
	11. Grip truck rental		$2,400
	20. Limousine (star)		2,400
	21. Rental trailer		3,000
	23. Expenses preproduction		2,000
		Subtotal:	$9,800

3600	Location Expenses		
	30. Preproduction		$ 2,000
	32. Catered meals		10,000
	33. Miscellaneous		2,500
	40. Location rentals		18,000
	41. Fire safety officer		900
		Subtotal:	$33,400

4400	Optical		
	11. Optical		$5,000
		Subtotal:	$5,000

4500	Editing		
	01. Supervising editor		$29,000
	02. Assistant editor		11,000
	03. Sound editor		8,000
	04. Music editor		2,400
	11. Coding		2,000
	14. Projection (dailies)		3,800
	16. Purchasing		2,000
	17. Equipment rental		12,000
		Subtotal:	$70,200

4600	Music		
	01. Composer, conductor, musicians, recording		$50,000
		Subtotal:	$50,000

4700	Postproduction		
	11. Sound transfer		$12,000
	12. Magnetic film		18,800
	13. Foley		5,100
	15. Sound FX		2,400
	20. Music recording		5,000

	21. Dolby stereo mixing		34,000
	25. Dialog recording		4,488
		Subtotal:	$81,788

4800	Film and Laboratory		
	08. 35mm raw stock		$17,600
	09. Developing		11,000
	10. Printing		14,000
	11. Negative cutting		6,200
	12. Sound negative dolby		4,140
	14. Answer prints		8,520
	15. Release prints		8,520
	85. Coding		2,000
	89. Tax		6,039
		Subtotal:	$78,019

6500	Publicity		
	01. Unit publicist		$10,000
		Subtotal:	$10,000

6700	Insurance		
	01. Cast, crew ($5 million)		
	02. Negative film, errors, and omissions; faulty stock, camera, and equipment; third-party property damage, workers' comprehensive and umbrella liability		
		Subtotal:	$54,000

6800	General Expenses		
	11. Telephone		$3,000
	12. Xerox		500
	13. Location accountant		5,000
	14. Office supplies		500
	15. Office costs		500
		Subtotal:	$9,500

7800	Indirect Cost		
	A. Cost overrun acct.		68,375
	B. Commission (10%)		250,000
		Subtotal:	318,375
		Total:	$2,500,124

Risk-Return. It is imperative that you are absolutely frank with your prospective investors. Naturally, you are eager for them to invest in your project, and you are almost certain that your film, special as it is, will not only return their investment but will also earn them a handsome profit.

Don't promise any castles in Spain. Your film has to go through many stages; it has to clear a number of hurdles to reach its break-even point. Make your investors aware that investing in a movie is a high-risk proposition and that they could suffer the total loss of their investment. Granted, legally you are not required to add a risk clause to your offering, but morally you are.

In discussing any potential returns, you must make it clear to your investors that you are not guaranteeing any returns. No one can predict a film's profit or loss. The success or failure of any film depends largely on the audience's reaction and the existing worldwide political and economic situation at the time of the movie's release. It is, therefore, an unrealistic practice—regardless how often employed—to compare one's project with similar films that are presently, or have been recently, on the market. One has to take into consideration that audiences' reactions are unpredictable, and that the rule of thumb—comedies and escapist entertainment sell well in troubled times, while dramatic films do better in emotionally calmer periods—does not necessarily hold true. Nevertheless, do acquaint your prospective investors with the following lucrative sources of income (both domestically and foreign):

Theatrical release (domestic)
TV network sale (domestic)
Cable sale (domestic)
Home video sale (domestic)

Theatrical release (worldwide)
TV, cable, home video sales (worldwide)*

Book about film (if applicable)

Merchandising—toys, games, outfits (if applicable)

Next you may present your investors with a hypothetical cost-income scenario based upon your film's budget. The following scenario is based on

---

*The difference between domestic and worldwide sales will be discussed in the chapter on distribution.

an overall cost of $2,500,000. This budget in today's market denotes a low-budget project that has been produced primarily for home video and all areas of foreign distribution.

Impress upon your investors the fact that the given scenario is a hypothetical one, and should not be employed as a basis for any risk-return assessment.

> *Production Cost.* $1,725,000 above- and below-the-line cost.
> 400,000 production company's participation in
> P&A (prints and advertising)

Possibly your investors have not funded your project directly, but have supplied you with letters of credit (LC), which guarantee that investors will pay back the bank loan in case of the producer's default. In short, an LC gives you the opportunity to borrow money from a bank (more about LCs in chapter 8). Borrowing money from a bank will add about a 15 percent interest rate to your film's cost. And remember, you'll have to pay until the loan interest has been paid off, which, if the film has no legs, may take several years. Furthermore, depending on the economic situation at the time of the loan approval, your interest rate may be higher or lower than the hypothetical 15 percent. The sum of $375,000 interest reflects interest payment for one year. You will, without any doubt, save money if you withdraw money only as needed.

Income. $100,000—domestic theatrical release.

The scenario assumes that the production company hires a distributor to distribute the picture *domestically.* (As we'll find out later on, in the chapter on distribution, such a limited domestic theatrical release is of utmost importance for the film's cable, home video, and foreign [all areas] release.) The shockingly small amount of $100,000 refers to the production company's take after the exhibitor's* *share* and distributor's *fees* have been deducted.

> $1,500,000—domestic cable, negative pick-up
> 500,000—domestic home video, negative pick-up

A negative pick-up means that the cable and/or home video distribution company pays one-quarter of the agreed-upon amount upon delivery of the

*Exhibitors will be discussed in the chapter on distribution.

picture, and the rest in quarterly installments. Domestic cable will insist upon a *window,* a time period in which the film cannot be marketed in home video retail stores.

$400,000—TV rights
 250,000—TV syndication rights

Payments of TV and TV syndication rights dribble in within about five years, as your film will be sold for areas as a "package" with other films.

$1,000,000—foreign rights worldwide

The above foreign incomes have been calculated after distribution fees and related expenses have been deducted.

Our hypothetical scenario gives us the following income picture.

Cost $2,500,000
Income   3,100,000

This is the income to be earned during the picture's first year. The second year will see some insignificant worldwide income, whereas the film will bring about $650,000 during the following five-year period.

After the initial investment has been paid back the investor will share the first year's profit of $600,000—and the following profit of $650,000—with you.

As far as the scenario is concerned, be advised of the following:

- The scenario reflects that the producer hires a distributor (we will discuss the pros and cons of such practice in the chapter on distribution).
- That the investors provided the producer with LC only (if they choose direct investment, they save a bundle on interest rates).
- The given scenario reflects cost and income at the time of writing (these amounts, all based on supply and demand, change from year to year).
- Do not get tied down in guaranteeing profits.

Fiscal control. Specify that all funds obtained from investors will be held in escrow until the needed sum has been raised. If the producer should fail to raise the required sum within a given period, monies collected will be returned without interest. Once the production is under way, a production accountant of the investor's choice will handle the daily expenditures and will supply the investor with weekly financial reports.

Investor's protection. Since a number of independently produced films are not completed, some investors insist upon a *completion bond.* A completion bond is expensive, and many low-budget films do not qualify to apply for one. (The firm issuing the bond guarantees the completion of the film, in case the production goes over budget.) In any event, with or without a completion bond, you should point to your team's (producer, production manager, director) track record, to satisfy any investor that the production will be completed.

Overcall. No *overcall* (monies needed should the film go over budget) will be collected from investors. The general partners may advance or borrow funds to be repaid prior to the returns due to the limited partnership. The respective percentage interest of each partner will NOT be affected.

Share of profits. It is mandatory that you inform your prospective investors that profits are not to be shared until after the costs of the film have been paid back to the investors. The traditional profit participation is 50/50, that is to say, 50 percent of the profits go to the investors and 50 percent of the profits go to the producer. Investors share their profits based on the percentage level of investment. Profits will be shared on net profits only. (Later, we will discuss the delicate balance between net profit and gross profit, since accounting concepts do vary from distributor to distributor and studio to studio.)

The traditional view that a picture has to bring in three to four times its cost before a new profit will be achieved, refers to *studio*-financed and -distributed films. The average low-budget film, employing a distributor for hire and contracting with a representative for worldwide distribution, enjoys net profits much sooner.

Marketing. Your marketing information has to support the financing program you have outlined. It contains:

1. Your film's promotable elements
2. Advertising and publicity
3. Concept viability
4. Suggested distribution plan

1. *Promotable elements.* A list of all of your film's promotable elements (stars, director, story).

2. *Advertising and publicity*. Explain the advertising and publicity tools you plan to employ. Having already contracted a well-known PR firm helps. Concentrate, as discussed in chapter 1, on advertising and promotional tools appropriate to your film's genre. It's an excellent strategy to attach samples of one-sheets and sales flyers (to be distributed at the international film markets) and, if you primarily go after the home video audience, cassette box covers, as well. Remember the old proverb "A picture is worth a thousand words," and give your potential investors a visual idea of the planned movie.

3. *Concept viability*. Much has been written and even more has been said during the past years about a film's viability. Much money has been spent on researching the "moviegoing market" based on family income, sex, and regional aspects. The research suggests that a larger number of mature people are available for theater attendance, but that mature *young people* constitute the important swing that can make a movie a hit.

Very well, that's this year's conclusion, but will it hold true for next year and the years to come? Who knows? When we consider the fact that it takes at least one year from the commencement of the screenplay to the release date of a film, we know that the applied research is yesterday's news and might not necessarily be applicable to your project.

It is far better to acquaint your investor with the film's intended target audience:

Art theater sophisticated audience
General release
Cable release
Home video release
Worldwide (all areas release)

Most likely your film has been targeted for a combination of release areas.

4. *Suggested distribution plan*. Ideally you'll have a distribution plan for your picture. But since no distribution company, even if it signed a letter of intent, will commit more fully to your project by establishing a distribution plan, you'll have to steer clear of specifics and remain on general terms. The following distribution plan is based upon our previous scenario of a film budget for $2,500,000:

• The film will be ready for release early fall.

- The film will be distributed on a limited domestic theatrical run; 50 prints during the months of September, October, November (these months are generally favorable for this type of film, as they do not interfere with the major summer and Christmas releases).
- The film will be shown on cable.
- The film will be exhibited at the major film markets (MIFED, Milan, Italy, October; Los Angeles Film Festival, Los Angeles, California, February; Cannes Film Festival, Cannes, France, April for all foreign rights sales).
- The film will be shown on TV, and syndicated TV.

Prospectus

While you need an offering to attract investors, you will submit a prospectus if you are interested in a studio deal.

Cover page
Highlights
Story synopsis
Story outline
Script
Promotional hook
Shortened version of budget
Producer's résumé

While it is mandatory that you present the studio with a final script and budget (once a studio accepts your project, both script and budget will undergo numerous changes), it is wise not to submit letters of intent from either stars or director. You may, however, suggest some names. Always keep in mind that studio executives have their own ideas about stars and directors who are "simply perfect" for this film.

The following is an example of a typical prospectus. The prospectus of my low-budget horror film *Frozen Scream* has been attached.

Ciara Productions, Inc.

A California Corporation*
Chill Factor
A Motion Picture Project

Renée Harmon, president
Address
Telephone Number

*You do not have to be incorporated to submit a project to a studio.

Highlights

THE PROGRAM

Ciara Productions, Inc. intends to produce a film with the current working title *Chill Factor* (the motion picture).

The original screenplay has been written by Renée Harmon. The film will be produced by Renée Harmon (the producer). Producer has a history of bringing her films in on schedule and within budget. Each of the producer's films has returned a profit. Producer is experienced and has demonstrated her ability to provide or obtain essential supporting cast and crew suitable to needs of this production. Producer's track record shows ability to deliver film on schedule and within budget. The producer has committed to bring the film in on time and within the budget.

The Motion Picture
The motion picture, a full-length feature film, is to be produced from the original screenplay by the working title *Chill Factor*. It is to be filmed in 35mm.

Project Status
SCRIPT: The script has been written. Script may be revised or polished in preproduction.

LEGAL STATUS: The production and creative team, including but not limited to, producer, director, writer, editor, etc. are to be considered independent contractors.

Sample: Story Synopsis

This story deals with the occult concept of age-old entities prolonging their lives indefinitely by taking over, and inhabiting, human bodies.

At the small Southern California college of South Coast University two scientists, Sven Jonson and Lil Stanhope, are convinced that by keeping a person's body temperature close to the freezing point, human life can be extended to near immortality.

Their assistant Tom Gerard dies of a heart attack. His wife, Ann, suspects he was murdered. No one believes her except Detective McGuire, who, nonplussed by the previous disappearance of two of Sven's students, eagerly helps her to find the murderer. He is sure that Sven Jonson is the culprit; he is also sure that some gruesome experiments took place.

Matters become more complicated. Not only do McGuire and Ann fall in love but also Ann encounters Tom—or someone like Tom—alive. She is determined to find out about Tom's death or disappearance.

Sample: Story Outline

Tom Gerard is chairman of the psychology department of South Coast University, a small private college. He is young and ambitious, and he has found the perfect partners for the breakthrough in longevity (leading to immortality) he is hoping for. His partners are Sven Jonson and Lil Stanhope, psychiatrists with strong interests in biochemical research.

His wife, Ann, a brittle young woman, is troubled by the secrecy of her husband's work, although she understands it involves altering animal metabolism as a technique for retarding aging.

Upon returning home from a Midsummer Eve party, Ann finds her husband dead. She is told that Tom had a heart attack, but she believes Tom has been murdered. She suspects Sven to be the killer. Ann has a breakdown. After several weeks in the hospital she returns home. Upon Lil's—her best friend—urging, she hires Tom's former assistant, the beautiful young Cathrine, as her nurse.

There is another mystery. Early in the summer two of Tom's students, Kirk and Bob, vanish. Detective Kevin McGuire of the San Luis police is under pressure to locate them. He suspects that drugs as well as criminal experiments on humans are involved in the case. He attempts to learn more from Ann about the nature of her husband's experiments. The two agree to collaborate. Soon they are following several promising leads. There are indications that the beautiful, young Cathrine is really an eighty-year-old woman, artificially kept young. Bob's landlady, Mrs. Gregory, reports of having seen Bob alive, if greatly changed in appearance. Ann is certain there is a secret lab where dark experiments take place. Yet every lead ends up on a dead-end street. There are logical explanations for everything, until Sven Jonson is found murdered. Now, in rapid succession, strange things begin to happen that make Ann suspect a dark force at work.

Through all of it, Lil stands by Ann in true friendship, and Ann's relationship with Kevin deepens. She knows she has fallen in love with him.

Ann has to live through a number of frightening experiences. On one occasion, she encounters Bob's apparition; twice she sees Tom's ghost. Shortly thereafter she recognizes a very-much-alive Bob in a supermarket and follows him to an abandoned cottage that—much to her surprise—is located in a straight line from Sven's mansion. Shortly after she has to flee her home, as it becomes invaded by unexplainable forces. She moves in with Mrs. Gregory. Visiting an antique market, she sees a man who she knows is Tom. That same evening Tom calls, asking her to meet with him. He promises to explain what is happening. Ann drives to Tom's apartment, which turns out to be a half-demolished tenement in Los Angeles. Ann follows Tom's voice from floor to floor, and she ends up in a dark room. Tom's voice turns out to be a tape-recorded message, and to her horror Ann discovers that had she taken another step she would have fallen to her death; she stands in front of a gaping hole in the wall.

Ann decides against telling Kevin about her experience. Things have changed. She does not trust him anymore. Neither does she trust her friend Lil any longer. Lil has drawn the man Ann loves into the circle of her unexplainable power. And, in a mysterious way Ann feels her own strength and will weaken. She knows she will be Lil's next victim, and she also knows the day of her death will be Lil's Summer's End party.

Lil tells her, gleefully, that she is a witch. It was she who has murdered Tom as well as Sven, as both men came too close to the true secret of her power: immortality. Lil's explanation pulls Ann out of her almost catatonic state. An inner force commands her to expose Lil. The only chance to do so, she knows, is to find the secret lab. She remembers the ruins of the old house that is located above Sven's mansion. She assumes that a tunnel connects the ruin, Sven's mansion, and the abandoned cottage. Somewhere in between, she suspects, must be the lab. She finds the entrance to the tunnel and fights her way through it but finds no secret lab. Yet in the root cellar of the cottage she discovers a huge freezer. Here she finds the frozen bodies of Lil's victims, now mindless and soul-less robots. Tom and Cathrine are among the robots. Ann takes photos and is about to leave when one of the corpses, Bob, becomes animated. Ann escapes. Bob chases her. Ann finds refuge in an old factory building. She calls the police and hides. A man enters the building. It is Bob.

Bob is ready to kill Ann by injection when Lil arrives and intervenes. She begs Ann to join forces with her and help with the project of immortality. Yes, she admits, the masses of people will be robots without emotions and wills of their own. Only a few intellects will receive the gift of true immortality, and those will rule the world. Ann refuses Lil's offer. Lil is ready to kill her, when Kevin and a few FBI men arrive on the scene. Ann by now is convinced that Kevin is part of the deadly game Lil had been playing all along. But her fears prove to be false. Kevin arrests Lil for murder. The moment the handcuffs touch her wrists Lil begins to age—her hair turns white, her features sag, she becomes an old, old woman. Next her flesh falls off her bones, until her skull is revealed, and then suddenly she shoots up in flames.

Kevin explains to Ann that he is an important FBI official. He had been informed about criminal experiments at South Coast, and had sent two of his most experienced agents, Bob and Kirk, to investigate. They were under-cover pretending to be students. When both agents vanished, he decided to investigate the case himself. Ann was one of his prime suspects. True, he met her to find out about the experiments, but soon he fell in love with her. His proposal was not part of the game; he loves her and wants to marry her.

Ann listens to Kevin, but his words do not touch her heart. She walks out of the room. Kevin goes after her, but in the hallway he runs past her. Ann knows she is invisible. She is not surprised about it. She walks all night long. And as she walks Lil's secret reveals itself to her. Lil was not a witch, she was a human body housing an age-old entity, and this entity has inhab-ited human bodies from time immemorial. She has flashes of memories that are not her own, but the ones of the immortal entity that has taken over her body.

Sample: Promotional Hook

When Ann discovers her husband Tom murdered, she goes into shock. Everyone tries to convince her that Tom died of a heart attack, but her nightmarish visions lead her to believe otherwise. Her curiosity brings her to a secret laboratory where she finds him, a frozen zombie.

Many films promise terror, but this is truly frightening.

Sample: Script

CHILL FACTOR (WORKING TITLE)

Exterior Country Road. Night.
A lonely country road pelted by sheets of rain. The camera takes in the dim outline of a small building sheltered by trees. A red neon sign flashing through the darkness designates the building as the Dew Drop Inn.

The headlights of a car cut through the rain. A car approaches and stops in front of the inn. PULL IN as Ann, a young woman, gets out of her car. PAN with her, as she walks to a public phone situated at the side of the building.

PULL IN to MEDIUM, as Ann fishes in her purse for a coin. The heavy rain makes her task difficult. She shivers in her lightweight cotton dress, pushes her wet mane of red hair out of her face, finally finds the coin, deposits it, and dials.

> ANN
> Tom, I'm sorry . . . but I'm a little late. . . .

Exterior Tom Gerard's House. Night.
A small, Victorian house, its outline—the veranda and the turret—are barely visible in the rain.

> VO ANN
> . . . you know how Sven is . . .

DIFFERENT ANGLE. A shadowy figure slips around the corner of the house, hesitates for a moment, then looks up.

> VO ANN
> . . . once he starts talking, he finds no end. But
> after all, he is your boss . . .

The shadowy figure's POV, a lighted window.

>   VO ANN
>   . . . and since you did not want to attend his
>   Midsummer Night's party . . .

Interior Tom Gerard's House. Study.
A book-lined study. The corners of the room are steeped in shadows, only a lamp on Tom's desk spills a pool of light on his face. He is in his middle thirties, kind of ascetic looking.

>   TOM
>   Honey, you didn't have to trek out in this
>   weather. You ought to have stayed at Lil's. . . .

Dimly the sound of humming voices comes up. Tom looks over his shoulder.

>   TOM
>   You shouldn't have left because of me.

Exterior Inn. Telephone. Night.
MEDIUM on Ann

>   ANN
>   You sounded so strange this afternoon, just before
>   I left.

Interior Tom Gerard's House. Study. Night.

>   TOM
>   I was just a little upset. I'm all right now . . . really
>   I am.

The sound of the humming voices increases.

>   VO ANN (filtering through)
>   If you really want to know, I was feeling a little
>   homesick for you. . . .

Exterior Inn. Telephone. Night.

> ANN
>
> I love you so, Tom. . . .
> I'll love you forever . . .

Interior Tom Gerard's House. Study. Night.
Tom sits very still, as if frozen.

> VO ANN
>
> . . . and ever . . . see you soon.

> TOM (with difficulty)
>
> Yes, hon, real soon.

Exterior Inn. Telephone. Night.

> ANN
>
> I love you.

She hangs up, turns, and walks toward her car.

CU SHOCK ZOOM the car lights. Sound of humming voices, suddenly interspersed with the sound of a clock ticking.

Interior Tom Gerard's House. Night.
CU on clock ticking, louder and louder; the dial shows about two minutes to midnight.

Finally Tom puts the receiver back into its cradle. He looks at the telephone. After a while he picks up Ann's picture.

CU on Ann's picture.

CU on Tom, as he reacts to his wife's picture.

Exterior Tom's House. Night.
PAN with the shadowy figure walking to the door.

MEDIUM on figure, its face hidden by a black hood; a hand reaches out. CU on hand turning the doorknob.

Interior Tom Gerard's House. Study. Night.
CU on hand dialing a telephone number.

PULL BACK to TIGHT MEDIUM on Tom.

> TOM
> Hello? This is Dr. Gerard again. Is Father O'Brian back from the church yet? Any minute? Yes, well please have him call me as soon as he arrives. Tell him it's urgent . . . life or death.

Tom hangs up, hesitates, then opens a desk drawer.

CU on Tom's hand reaching for a gun.

Back on TOM. He checks to see whether the gun is loaded, and it is. He puts the gun in front of him. The SOUND OF HUMMING VOICES has decreased somewhat, but all of a sudden the sound of a CLOCK TICKING cuts through the HUMMING VOICES, louder and louder.

(The rhythm becomes faster; cross cutting adds to the increasing speed of the scene.)

Suddenly the phone rings. Tom, relief on his face, answers.

> TOM
> Father O'Brian, thank God, I can't hold off any longer, it's happening tonight . . . and . . . he'll . . . Who is this?

There is a long pause. Then a husky voice answers.

> VO VOICE
> The angels will be there in a few moments. Be ready for them.

The phone clicks off. Sound of hollow dial tone.

Exterior Inn. Night.
Ann approaches her car, gets in, slams door shut.

Interior Tom Gerard's House. Hallway. Night.
TIGHT MEDIUM on black-clad arm, hand closes the front door ever so carefully. PULL BACK to reveal a black-clad, hooded figure.

Interior Tom Gerard's House. Study. Night.
Tom grabs his gun.

Interior Tom Gerard's House. Staircase. Night.
CU on feet walking upstairs (flashcut).

CU of hand on banister (flashcut).

Interior Tom Gerard's House. Study. Night.
Tom is on the phone, his voice thick with fear.

> TOM
> Beach Station? Give me Sgt. McGuire right
> away. . . . Yes . . . please . . . Tom Gerard . . .

Exterior Road. Night.
On Ann's car, speeding; her headlights cut ribbons of light through the rain.

Interior Tom Gerard's House. Upper Hallway. Night.
CU on feet walking.

Interior Tom Gerard's House. Study. Night.

> TOM
> . . . it's an emergency . . . tell him . . .

Tom is interrupted by the sound of heavy footsteps. He drops the receiver, hurries to the door.

He throws the door to the hallway open.

Interior Tom Gerard's House. Upper Hallway. Night.
Tom's POV. The empty hallway.

INSERT the phone receiver dangling.

> VO MCGUIRE
> Hello, Tom . . . Tom . . . answer me. . . .

CLOSE ANGLE on Tom standing motionless at the top of the stairs. Sweat builds on his temples, as he listens for a sound . . . any sound. Yet the night remains deadly quiet.

Tom descends the stairway cautiously.

ANGLE on Tom's gun pointed straight ahead.

ANGLE on Tom stopping at the bottom of the stairs. He breathes heavily as he checks around for danger. LOW LIGHTING of heavy shadows, the possibility of lurking danger, ready to strike.

Suddenly there is a whisper.

> VO VOICE
> Time to pay your debts to science, Tom Gerard.

Tom whirls around.

His POV. At the head of the stairs, bathed in blinding white light, stands the hooded figure.

Titles begin to roll

Sample: Budget

At the inital stage of contracting a studio, a shortened version of your budget will suffice. Needless to say, the sample budget given is too small to interest any major studio in the proposed film. Since, however, our film *Frozen Scream* (working title *Chill Factor*) obviously was a low-budget film (the film was distributed by the independent company 21st Century Distribution), I feel that a comparative budget ought to be given as a sample. The following is the shortened version of the budget listed in the offering.*

BUDGET

1100	Story and Rights	$ 30,500
1200	Producer's Unit	182,000
1300	Direction	58,000
1400	Star	1,000,000
	Supporting Cast	80,300
1500	Agent's Fees	108,030
1900	Above-Line Fringe Benefits	138,162
2000	Production Staff	19,000
2200	Set Design	21,200
2300	Set Construction	2,000
2500	Set Operation	21,900
2600	Special Effects	950
2700	Set Dressing	1,200
2800	Petty Cash	1,200
2900	Wardrobe	7,100
3100	Makeup and Hair Dressing	7,800
3200	Lighting	28,200
3300	Production Sound	17,300
3400	Camera	58,200
3500	Transportation	9,800
3600	Location Expenses	33,400
4400	Opticals	5,000
4500	Editing	70,200
4600	Music	50,000

*The given budget does not reflect the actual budget of our film *Frozen Scream*.

4700	Postproduction—Sound	81,788
4800	Laboratory (developing and printing)	75,019
6500	Publicity	10,000
6700	Insurance	54,000
6800	General Expenses	9,500
7800	Indirect Cost	318,375
		Total: $2,500,124

Sample: Producer's Résumé

Renée Harmon

Renée Harmon produced and wrote the screenplays for the following motion pictures:

Jungle Trap	World Inter Media Distribution, Palace International, Korea Raidon Home Video, USA, 1991
Revenge	World Inter Media Distribution, Palace International, Korea Raidon Home Video, USA, 1991
Red Satchel	Schau Mal Home Video, Germany, 1990
Escape from the Insane Asylum	Cinevest Entertainment Group, USA and Overseas, 1989
Run Coyote Run	World Inter Media Group, USA and Overseas, 1988
Night of Terror	Video Pictures Distribution, Mid American Home Video, USA, 1987
Executioner II	21st Century Distribution, Worldwide, Continental Home Video, USA, 1986
Hellriders	21st Century Distribution, Worldwide, Transworld Home Video
Frozen Scream	21st Century Distribution, 1985
Lady Streetfighter	Scope II Distribution, USA, 1982

3.

From literary property to screenplay: what you need to know to acquire and create a promotable concept

No movie can be offered and subsequently produced without its basic requirement: the *property*. The property can be a stage play, novel, short story, nonfiction essay, newspaper, or magazine article. Regardless of the source of your property you, the producer, have to make certain that you hold the right to the property.

You must *option* the literary property. The option agreement states the option fee and the purchase price, as well as the time period during which the producer has the exclusive right to the property. To option a property you'll have to pay between 5 and 10 percent of its purchase price. Each additional option fee should be based upon the original one. Whether these option payments may be deducted from the eventual purchase price is open to negotiation.

Remember one important fact: The producer must option the property, and money—even if it is only one dollar—*has* to be exchanged. A handshake won't do. A little-known actuality is the convention that "who owns the property owns the project." Consequently, even though the author will not interfere with your developing the property, he or she is at liberty to interfere with your choice of star, director, location, and so on.

Therefore, prior to optioning any property you should understand exactly what the "producer's rights" are.

1. First, make certain that the author owns the property. Who has retained the copyright? The author or the publishing company? Who has retained the motion picture rights? If in doubt, search the Copyright Office in Washington, D.C. The motion picture rights to the property must be acquired from the party holding these rights.

2. The producer has the right to develop the property, that is to say, he/she will have the screenplay written, work on the budget, contact directors and stars, negotiate with distribution companies, and obtain publicity for the project.

3. The producer has the right to change elements (plot, characters, locations) of the literary property. (Sadly, this is the point of most contention—and often litigation—between author and producer. It is also the reason that at times a movie based upon a well-loved book disappoints us once we see it on the screen.) Incidentally, the right to change the plot and characterization does not apply to a stage play. A stage play must be presented word for word as written. And this, again, is the reason that a filmed play remains a play in every respect and often lacks the reality we associate with a film.

The Literary Purchase Agreement

I cannot stress enough that no producer, regardless how experienced, should either write or accept a literary purchase agreement unless he or she has consulted a well-versed entertainment attorney. There are several ways to find the entertainment attorney who's right for you (don't forget, attorneys' fees do vary widely):

Ask your attorney for a referral.

Call your local Bar Association.

Contact: Volunteer Lawyers for the Arts
  1560 Broadway, Suite 711
  New York, NY 10036

An entertainment attorney should check the literary purchase agreement, or even better, *write* it; after all, contracts and agreements are the entertainment attorney's field of expertise.

This brings me to "boilerplate"—those contract forms one buys in any stationery store specializing in motion picture and publishing forms. Boilerplate or model contracts—since they open the door to all kinds of legal loopholes—simply won't do.

The purchase agreement becomes effective as soon as the option is exercised. There is no set rule about the amount to be paid for the property. (This does not apply to the purchase agreement for a screenplay written by a member of the Writers Guild of America. We will discuss the WGA rules and regulations later on, as we deal with the screenplay per se.) For a literary property (book, article, short story, newspaper, or magazine account), the purchase price may be as small as a few hundred dollars, or it may skyrocket into millions.

The following are the most salient points any literary purchase agreement must contain:

1. Title of literary property.
2. Author's name, address, and social security number; WGA membership number if applicable.
3. Publisher of book, short story, or magazine/newspaper article.
4. Copyright information.
5. Purchase price.
6. The right to exhibit a film based upon said property in theaters.
7. The right to exhibit a film based upon said property nontheatrically, such as:
   Home video
   Cable
   TV
   Institutions, ships, airplanes, oil rigs, university, and school campuses.
8. The right to:
   Publish the screenplay issuing from said property in book form.
   Novelize (unless based upon novel) the motion picture based upon said property.
   Publish stills of the film based upon said property in book form.
9. The right to broadcast excerpts of the film based upon said property via radio (this right authorizes the producer to advertise the film via radio).
10. The right to publish the films, based upon said property, songs, and score.

11. The right to merchandise items (toys, T-shirts, posters) bearing the likeness of characters appearing in the film based upon said property.
12. The right to produce the film based upon said property for TV or cable in lieu of the planned theatrical production.
13. The right to publish synopsis of story content of film based upon said property for promotional purposes in newspapers and magazines.
14. The right to option any sequels of said literary property.
15. The right to withhold a part of the author's payment until after the film's release, since it is impossible to detect whether any literary property contains infringing material.
16. The right to assign rights in the literary property to third parties. Any bank or investment group financing your picture will *insist* that the literary property be assigned to them. (Remember: The one who owns the literary property, owns the project.)

A Look at Author's Rights

So far we have viewed the purchase of literary property from the producer's point of view. Yet I feel it is only fair to concern ourselves with the author's rights as well; after all, you, the producer, want a fair deal for all. Besides, this segment will help readers who are authors *and* producers.

The author may be asked to sign a *grant of rights* in lieu of the more traditional option. The grant specifies:

Payment for the initial grant.
Purchase price for the literary property. Reversion of the property to the author in case the producer fails to pay the payment for the initial grant.

Payment of purchase price for the literary property.

Reversion of property to author (or holder of copyright) in case the producer fails to pay the agreed-upon purchase price.

It is the last clause that makes the grant of rights agreement tricky. If the production company, after having paid part of the purchase price, goes into bankruptcy, then the literary property becomes *part of the production firm's assets*.

Since the author has to wait in line with all the other creditors, his/her property may be tied up for years.

It is for this reason that I advise the author to choose the traditional option.

In addition the author should retain the rights to any sequels of his/her property, as well as the rights to use the original property's characters, names, and location for sequels, and any literary property not connected to the property optioned.

The author should request that the following clauses be included in the literary purchase agreement:

1. A definite purchase price.

2. A definite payment schedule:

> Partial payment to begin at the commencement of preproduction.
> Partial payment at commencement of principal photography.
> Partial payment at delivery of answer print.
> Final payment after commencement of domestic release.

3. An *outright date,* a time that payment is due, even though the film has not commenced shooting. (Be aware that a film's date of principal photography might be delayed indefinitely.)

4. Your credits should read:

From the _____ by _____. They have to appear on the front titles on the same title card with the screenplay writer's name.

In case your contract stipulates that you, the author, will receive net profits, make certain that these net profits are in concert with the net profits earned by producer, director, and stars. An author's net profits should *never* be deducted from the producer's net profits.

How to Find a Terrific Screenwriter

You have optioned a screenplay and wish to have a screenplay written, or you may be in the market for an original screenplay—in short, you need a screenwriter. Unless you like being bombarded with, and finally suffocated by, an avalanche of poorly written screenplays do not advertise for one in any of the trade papers, or even worse, your local newspaper. You may, however, decide upon one of the following:

1. If you have optioned a literary property that is destined to become a major studio deal (and if you have the funds to pay a hefty advance), your best bet is to contact one of the Big Four: William Morris, CAA, ICM, and Triad.

The William Morris Agency
151 El Camino Drive
Beverly Hills, CA 90028

CAA
1888 Century Park East, #1400
Los Angeles, CA 90067

ICM
(International Creative Management)
8899 Beverly Boulevard
Los Angeles, CA 90048

Triad Artists
10100 Santa Monica Boulevard, 16th Floor
Los Angeles, CA 90067

Since Hollywood still seems to be the hub of the motion picture industry you may want to contact a number of smaller but highly respected and well-established agencies, such as:

Robinson-Weintraub-Gross & Assoc.
8428 Melrose #C
Los Angeles, CA 90069

Paul Kohner Inc.
9169 Sunset Boulevard
Los Angeles, CA 90060

The Lantz Office
9255 Sunset Boulevard #505
Los Angeles, CA 90069

Mitchell J. Hamilburg
292 S. La Cienega Boulevard, #212
Beverly Hills, CA 90211

The Gage Group
9229 Sunset Boulevard, #306
Los Angeles, CA 90069

Or you may contact the Writers Guild of America West for a list of agencies:

Writers Guild of America West
8955 Beverly Boulevard
West Hollywood, CA 90048

Needless to say, if you plan to employ a WGA writer, your company has to be signatory with WGA. That is to say, your company agrees to abide by WGA rules and pay scales. Even if you have not yet formed your company, you'll still have to sign a WGA agreement. This contract must be signed up front,

The screenwriter has to be paid for his/her services. No writer may write on spec [speculation]—the promise of future payments. The payment schedules vary and are subject to negotiation. Usually the writer receives a specified amount at the commencement of his/her work, additional payments for each rewrite, and the final payment either upon delivery of the final script and/or at the time of the movie's release.

The producer must pay basic scale. This scale varies, and the producer should get in contact with the local chapter of WGA to determine current rates. At the time of this writing the following royalty scale was in effect:

$25,000—basic minimum scale for a full-length feature film script.

$25,000—basic scale for a full-length feature film script for cable.

For the theatrical film the WGA writer receives residuals for TV network and TV syndicated exhibition, as well as cable sales. For home video sales the WGA writer receives royalties. These royalties are to be negotiated, and are based upon the number of cassettes *purchased,* while residuals depend on the number of times the film is *being shown on the small screen.*

For TV the following minimum pay scale applies at the time of this writing:

$21,359 for each one-hour segment of a miniseries and/or movie of the week.

$14,560 for each half-hour series episode (prime-time); $7,529 (syndicated).

A royalty of 20 percent of the initial fee paid for up to five reruns. No royalties are due after the fifth rerun. For syndication, a royalty of 10 percent applies.

In addition to the fee paid to the screenwriter, the producer has to pay WGA specified amounts for health and retirement plans.

If the writer wrote the original screenplay (one that is not based on a literary property), he/she will retain the screenplay's publication rights, called "separation rights." These rights, however, cannot be exercised until six months after the picture's release. The producer, however, retains the rights to publicize promotional synopses.

A producer signatory to WGA is free to hire a screenwriter who is not signatory to WGA, but a WGA signatory writer cannot work for a nonsignatory producer.

You should also take into consideration that pay scale and additional requirements and fringe benefits change whenever WGA negotiates a new contract.

2. As you can tell, contracting a top screenwriter is expensive. Still, the producer of limited means need not despair.

He or she can obtain an excellent screenplay for an honorarium below WGA basic scale by contacting:

DG
The Dramatists Guild
234 W. 44th Street
New York, NY 10036

3. There is no reason to believe that a nonunion writer's skills are inferior to a union counterpart's. Many talented and highly professional writers all across the country are nonunion for the simple fact that they have not as yet been hired by a WGA signatory production company. All these writers know their craft, are familiar with screenplay construction, and—happily and eagerly—will do a great job. You'll find such writers by contacting your local university's or college's cinema department. Ask for the instructor who teaches screenplay writing and enlist his or her help in finding a graduating student well versed in screenplay structure, and who possibly might have written a viable screenplay. Do not get pawned off to the English department.

True, English majors may have learned to write stage plays, but they are as yet unfamiliar with a screenplay's stringent demands.

Possibly you may contact a local institution that teaches screenplay writing. But watch out: Some of the courses offered are excellent, while others are too short to be of any value to the students. These "screenplay writing made easy" sessions simply teach some basic facts about a complicated matter.

If you hire a nonunion writer, you may be able to defer his or her salary to commencement of the film, completion of the film, or the film's net profit.

Since a beginning producer's first venture most likely won't bring in any net profits, I think it is more honest to sign the writer on as partner in a joint venture partnership, rather than grant the writer net profit participation.

The Screenplay

This segment pertains to an original screenplay (a screenplay that is *not* based upon a literary property) as well as a screenplay derived from literary property.

After the literary property has been purchased, the producer assigns a screenwriter to write the screenplay. Sometimes the author will want to write the screenplay. (This request will be granted only if the author is a best-selling writer who has clout.)

One has to remember that screenplay writing is a craft all by itself; its techniques differ greatly from the writing skills necessary to write a novel or an article. Unfortunately, only a few authors (fiction and nonfiction) take the time and effort needed to learn the mechanics of screenplay writing. Therefore, it stands to reason that even though a famous author wrote the first draft based on a literary property, sooner or later a professional screenwriter will be assigned to the project.

A screenplay moves through the following stages:

TREATMENT

A synopsis of the plot; a short description of main characters and locations. The synopsis is about ten to fifteen pages in length.

FIRST-DRAFT SCREENPLAY

The scenes are fully written, and some dialog has been added. This is the time when director, star, and the distributor—if you have signed with one— will put in their "two cents' worth" of advice. This is the most harassing time for both the screenwriter and the producer. The distributor—understand-ably—is concerned about the promotable aspects of the project. The star worries about the effectiveness (read: size) of his or her part. The director has artistic considerations and the producer deals with budgetary fears.

It is now that a film based on an excellent literary property (or on an original screenplay) may lose its center core by splintering into various directions.

You are faced with the difficult and often thankless task of listening to all demands, of considering their merits, of sorting the chaff from the wheat, of discarding what obscures the screenplay, but most of all of keeping the script on a straight path, so as not to obliterate the literary (or original screen-play's) core.

A discussion about the importance of keeping the literary property's basic ideas intact may seem out of place in a book dealing with financing a movie, but financing your movie begins with the film's conception. If the basic idea of a film, because of additions and/or deletions, becomes obscure, you'll open the door to reshooting and reediting—both time- and money-consuming processes.

It is easy to lose a handle on your film's concept as you fight your way through the jungle of rewrites and refinements. Many of the suggested changes may be excellent. However, many terrific but isolated moments do not necessarily add up to an effective cinematic matrix. Remember to keep these few simple facts in mind when you are dealing with an avalanche of suggested changes:

1. *Basic Idea.* Has the property's basic idea been preserved?
2. *Intent.* What does the screenplay intend to show to the audience?
3. *Emotion.* What feelings should the screenplay evoke in the audience?
4. *Theme.* The theme keeps the movie's core together by clearly express-ing three main ideas:
   This movie is about _____
   This movie establishes a strong belief in _____
   This movie intends to prove _____

5. *Goal.*   The theme leads to an understanding of why the protagonist (hero) pursues his or her goal.

Has the main question, "Will _____ achieve _____" been clearly established and satisfactorily answered?

WHAT YOU NEED TO KNOW ABOUT STRUCTURE

The screenplay's structure keeps your audience's interest in the movie alive.

1. Have the *who* and *where* been established clearly? Some scripts make the mistake of revealing the *what* (what is going to happen) and *why* (the motive for the main character's actions) just a little too early. Yes, the audience must know about the *what* and *why,* but first it has to meet the main characters *(who)* before it will care about what is happening to them.

The relationship between the main characters *(who)* and their environment *(where)* should be made known as early as possible. It is their relationship that explains the *why.*

2. Does the script contain any *twists,* and are they placed correctly?
Twist at the end of Act I: An event occurs that sets up the main plot *(what)* and the main character's motives subplot *(why).* These motives lead to the protagonist's (hero's) goal and the antagonist's (villain's) countergoal. This twist asks the main question: "Will _____ achieve _____?"
Twist I in the middle of Act II: Keeps the story going, possibly turns it in a different direction and repeats the main question. *Twist II at the end of Act II:* Pulls the story toward Act III and to the plot's climax and denouement.

3. Does the *what* and *why* grow out of the relationship between the main characters, or has it been imposed upon them for the purpose of creating an exciting plot? The *what* and *why* sets the story in motion:
What the story is about determines the main plot and the film's line of action. *Why* determines the main characters' motives, leading to goal and countergoal. *Why* establishes the film's subplot, which examines the film's theme.

4. Is the subplot strong enough? The subplot reveals the "human element" of your story. It gives your story depth, keeps your characters from becoming "cardboard figures," and demands the audience's empathy. Here are some guidelines:

• The subplot must be part of the story, not a story by itself. While the main plot tells the story, the subplot focuses on the relationship between people. Often, the subplot is the stronger and more interesting one, but it is the plot that causes the actions the characters take, and as such holds the film together (in *Kramer vs. Kramer* the subplot deals with the couple's relationship to each other; the plot deals with the custody case).

• Once you have clarified your plot-subplot structure you will have to check the structure of the subplot: The subplot has the identical structure as the main plot; it has a beginning, a middle, and an end. It has twists of its own.

• The subplot twists should be placed as closely as possible to their respective main plot twists. If you are struggling with a script, most likely you are facing faulty main plot–subplot integrations.

The Middle (Act II). Act II is where your screenplay should develop into an increasingly gripping matrix. At times, unfortunately, Act II may drag after an interesting beginning (Act I). Besides main plot and subplot twists and the integration of both, you need the following to keep Act II alive:

Momentum
Graduation
Suspense
Foreshadowing
Dark moment
Highlight scenes
Obstacles and conflicts

Momentum. Momentum simply means that a story gains in strength. This is achieved by the application of graduation and suspense.

Graduation. Check your story. Are all events on the same high- or low-interest level, or do they vary in strength? Interest level must move up even though you should give your audience plateaus when "nothing much happens." Does the final (and highest) graduation lead into the dark moment and from there into the twist that propels the story into Act III?

Suspense. While graduation keeps the audience's interest alive, it is overlapping suspense that holds Act II together. Act II consists of a series of overlapping suspense sequences, each headed by a goal that has to be either frustrated or satisfied. The point is that a *new overlapping suspense sequence begins before the denouement of the previous one.*

Make certain that the suspense sequence B has been set before the denouement of suspense sequence A has been delivered.

The denouement of the various suspense sequences must be delivered at the end of Act II; then only the main question needs to be answered.

Never fail to make your character's expectations of the outcome clear to your audience. Remember, your audience expects some outcome. It is fun (and makes for an exciting film) to manipulate this expectation.

1. The denouement does not happen as anticipated—surprise.
2. The audience at this point does not expect a denouement—shock. (This technique was used to great effect in the original *Halloween.*)
3. The denouement happens as expected—satisfaction.

It is obvious that an always satisfied anticipation becomes as boring as a continually frustrated expectation becomes annoying.

Foreshadowing. Foreshadowing is another integral part of momentum. Any event needs to be foreshadowed twice. Audiences should not become aware of foreshadowing; they should remember, however, that the foreshadowed event has taken place.

Dark moment. The twist at the end of Act II features the dark moment, when everything seems lost. It is imperative that at this point the main plot and subplot twists are closely integrated, and that the main plot twist moves the story in a different direction. (The dark moment occurs in *Jungle Trap* when everyone but Chris and Leila has been killed.)

Highlight scenes. A highlight scene resembles a plot within a plot. The highlight scene is an excellent device that keeps the middle of a motion picture from dragging. It is most effective if it occurs immediately after the first twist.

1. The highlight scene ought to be an integral part of your film; it should not take off on a tangent of its own.

2. The highlight scene should not last more than five to seven minutes.
3. A highlight scene, starting from a point of departure, features a beginning (Act I), a middle (Act II), and an end (Act III). A twist occurs at the end of Act II.

Obstacles and conflicts. Obstacles are barriers that keep a character from reaching a goal. Obstacles are important because they give you, the beginning producer-director, the chance to "prove character in action," that is to say, characters have to react to obstacles in keeping with their established personality: A braggart will not react humbly; a sensible person will not turn reckless, unless the secondary trait of recklessness has been established (foreshadowed) prior to the event.

Obstacles are closely connected to *conflict.* All conflicts need to be established clearly; at times they need to be foreshadowed. Never expect your audience to guess who is in conflict with whom or what, *but spell it out.* Only three conflict patterns are possible: Man against man/woman; man against nature; and man against himself.

If your script lacks suspense, I recommend that you investigate the obstacle/conflict area. Ask yourself:

1. Has an obstacle or a conflict been established early enough to cause audience anticipation?

2. Do the opposing forces have an *equal chance* to reach their goal? If not, the script will lack *suspense.* If John and Jerry court Miss Beautiful, but all advantages are on John's side, no suspense is evoked. But if the chance of success is equally distributed between the two, then we, the audience, are interested in the outcome of the competition.

3. Are goal and countergoal clearly stated, and are both focused upon the same area? Mary and Beth are both up for the starring role in an Off-Broadway play. The girls are equally compelled to win the role, but they have never met, and they do not know of each other's existence—same goal, but no conflict, and therefore no suspense. But if Mary and Beth are friends and devious Beth does everything in her power to discredit sweet Mary, then we have a countergoal, conflict, and suspense.

The End (Act III). Do NOT: introduce any new characters or any new events.

End your subplot before the climax begins. The climax focuses on the *main plot only*.

But DO: let the climax build up swiftly, tie up all loose ends, and answer the main question.

DELIVERY OF THE FINAL SCRIPT

A word of warning: Even after a script has been polished (has had a final going-over), it should never be termed a "final script," as lines and scenes may be changed during shooting.

The considerate producer will give the screenwriter between three and six months from commencement of writing to delivery.

4.

Distribution:

a primer for professionals

The distribution game is complicated. It is a contract-driven game, where each aspect of a contract must hinge upon the next. No producer should venture into this game without having an experienced attorney and a knowledgeable accountant on his or her side. Distribution is a game that requires a team approach.

This chapter, and I cannot emphasize this enough, tries to give you some very basic knowledge about the ways distribution works, the pitfalls one might encounter, and the maze of various distribution practices. *In no way* does this chapter stand in lieu of any legal advice given by an attorney, or financial advice given by an accountant. This chapter shows the facts; it is up to your attorney and accountant to interpret them.

There are various ways to distribute a film. It is the distributor's responsibility to find the best one for your picture:

Distribution by saturation
Platform release
Limited engagement
Market-by-market saturation
Four-walling

DISTRIBUTION BY SATURATION

Only major studios can afford saturation, since as a blockbuster opens simultaneously in several thousands of theaters nationwide, it must be supported by enormous—and very expensive—national and local advertising.

The rationale is that the blockbuster must earn the greatest dollar amount in the shortest time period.

PLATFORM RELEASE

The same as its counterpart, the motion picture release by saturation, the film given a platform release opens *simultaneously* nationwide. But it opens in fewer theaters and usually in major cities only. From there the film moves into secondary markets, smaller towns, and smaller theaters. Advertising thrusts toward local newspaper, radio, and TV ads. The platform-released picture relies heavily upon the previously discussed press kit. Most major studios release their "run of the mill" film, as well as all films that have been picked up by a major studio-distributor on a platform-release basis.

LIMITED ENGAGEMENT

Such a film opens in just a few select theaters in Los Angeles, New York, and Chicago, and from there—if the audience response warrants it—makes its way into the other major markets.

Advertising for a limited-engagement film has to be geared to an identifiably sophisticated audience. Some major studios prefer to release films of artistic merit but limited audience appeal in this manner.

MARKET-BY-MARKET SATURATION

A film of special appeal to certain geographic areas and/or socioeconomic groups does best if distributed market-by-market. A rather small number of prints, rarely more than about two hundred, supported by adequate but not expensive local advertising, moves from territory to territory. Most independent distribution companies employ market-by-market distribution, by "farming" a picture out to territorial subdistributors. Both distributor and subdistributor (called "territorials") share the advertising cost. Of course, ultimately you, the producer, will pay for these. A film distributed market-by-market does not utilize any national advertising.

If a small number of prints have to be circulated, the producer might elect to bypass a distributor altogether by contracting subdistributors operating in various territories. These territorials do not necessarily distribute state by state. A California-based territorial, for instance, may service part of California, plus Arizona and Nevada. Most likely the territorial subdistributor requires that you advance most of the advertising cost.

FOUR-WALLING

In case a producer has been unable to interest neither independent distributor nor territorial subdistributor, the producer might consider four-walling by contacting theater owners directly. Areas can be worked one at a time with just a few prints. You'll have to supply all advertising, such as one-sheets, newspaper, mats, and—if warranted—radio blurbs. In a way, you *rent* the theaters by paying the exhibitor either via a specified rental amount or a certain percentage of the box office intake. Needless to say, such a practice does not work with any national theater chain such as Mann's or Loew's, or any of the privately owned multiplex theaters. Four-walling is a viable way of getting your picture into distribution, if you are dealing with one of the quickly disappearing mom-and-pop theaters. After deducting your advertising costs, I doubt whether you may break even by four-walling your movie. But, if you need a domestic release in order to gain a more lucrative home video contract, four-walling might be the way to go.

Now that we've discussed how to distribute your film, let's talk about where to distribute it.

Majors*

Before the Paramount consent decree, studios controlled distribution by owning theaters outright. Since then the major studios' influence on distribution has been somewhat diminished; still, they are "the big fish in the pond."

*Disney, Universal, Warner Bros., Paramount, Sony (Columbia), 20th Century Fox

After all, majors maintain nationwide and worldwide distribution networks, and they do run the distribution game. Certainly, every major studio finances and produces a number of films but picks up the majority of its releases from well-established production companies.

Since $20 million is the *average* budget for a film produced by a major studio, it is understandable that generally only well-known and well-connected producers who can show a track record of successful films will be given the opportunity to ally themselves with a major studio.

Yet, one never knows what will happen: A beginning producer who owns a terrific project might be able to interest a studio. Consequently, it is necessary to take a long and hard look at the "studio deal."

At this point you'll have to distinguish between the studio deal (a major studio finances and distributes a picture) and the "pick-up deal" (a major distributor agrees to distribute a film that had been financed by an outside source). In the first instance you, the producer, exchange most if not all artistic control for a lucrative salary; in the latter, you retain artistic control but have to take the chance that your investors might see no profit, and stand in danger of recovering possibly only a fraction of their investments.

Frankly, both the studio deal and "studio pick-up"—unless you have secured the now all but extinct "negative pick-up"*—are not quite as sweet as they seem. Still, the fact remains that seeing your film released by a major studio gives you and your picture the kind of prestige that will make it easier for you to negotiate a favorable distribution contract with one of the mini-majors, as you develop your second film.

The Formal PD Agreement (Production-Distribution Agreement)

A major studio requires that the producer enter into a production-distribution agreement, called the PD agreement.

The studio, fully aware of the fact that the financial opportunity is vested in distribution, will spend millions on your film to make millions more.

---

*Upon delivery of the film, the distributor pays and agrees upon the amount, usually some percentage above the film's production cost. Payments will be made in four quarterly installments.

First, a word of advice regarding the studio deal. If you have visions of sending your script directly to a major studio, forget it. Studios do not accept scripts from unknown producers or writers. There are only three ways to approach a studio:

1. Submit your script (not your offering) through a well-established agency.
2. Submit your offering (not your prospectus) to one of the big agencies (such as William Morris, CAA, ICM) that package projects.
3. Submit your *prospectus* (as discussed in chapter 2) directly to the major studio.

1. *Have your script (not your offering) submitted to a studio by a well-established agency.* Make certain that the agent under consideration not only has contacts in the motion picture industry, and will target your script only to these major studios and mini-majors, for which your script's genre is just right, but also target it to an executive with enough clout to start the process. Let me warn you, if your agent does not have strong connections, your script will end up in a studio's story department for evaluation. There an assigned reader synopsizes the submission and recommends the project for further consideration or rejection. Unfortunately, the majority of these readers are people on the first rung of their career ladder, who have not as yet developed the talent necessary to "sense" a viable project among the many less desirable or frankly amateurish ones they have to evaluate. Also, it is understandable that these readers hesitate to put their limited expertise on the line by recommending a project.

The scripts that have passed through the readers' "sieves" are submitted to the story department, where the story editor has a chance to either reject a script or move it on to the vice president in charge of production for further evaluation.

2. *Submit your offering (not your prospectus) to one of the big agencies (such as William Morris, ICM, or CAA) that package projects.*

Your project will have a fair chance of success if one of the big agencies handles the package, as the agent in charge (bypassing the story editor) gets in contact with the vice president of production. Furthermore, the big agencies know about the kind of projects currently demanded by majors and mini-majors.

And now a word about the package. First, submit your offering but not your prospectus. Agreed, the offering, having been tailored to attract investors, is not the document that the packager submits to the studios, but it gives an overview of your project, its costs, and possible commercial viability. At this point it is better not to have solicited any letters of interest from either director and/or stars (and positively no such letter from any distribution company; after all, the majors and mini-majors are not as much interested in producing your film as in distributing it). As far as actors and director are concerned, letters of interest present a severe hindrance. It is in the packager's interest to supply talent from his or her own pool of clients.

In turn, the packager writes a proposal, including those segments of your offering deemed important.

And in both cases, regardless of whether you work with an agent or a packager, you must sign a release before your script will be submitted.

3. *Submit your prospectus directly to the major studio and/or mini-major.* If you are in the very fortunate position of having the opportunity to submit your prospectus (not your offering) to a studio or mini-major, be advised *not* to suggest names of stars and directors. One studio's beloved star might be another one's deplorable monster. Patiently wait for the studio's casting suggestions.

And now, after this necessary detour, we'll go back to the major studio's production-distribution (PD) agreement.

Before entering into a PD agreement you must negotiate your position in the deal:

1. The producer (you) forms a corporation. It is the corporation, not the producer, who enters into the PD agreement with the studio.
2. The producer enters into the PD agreement with the studio.

(Please do not confuse the PD agreement with a distribution agreement; in the first the studio finances and distributes the picture; in the latter the studio only distributes the picture.)

And now let's illuminate the pros and cons of both situations:

The corporation enters into the PD agreement with the studio. Most likely, a producer entering a PD agreement with a major studio, being a well-known producer, already heads his or her own corporation. It is, however, at times far better to form a corporation for each individual of your studio-financed project. True, corporation status may limit tax advantages, but the benefits the producer gains from his or her corporation's status far outweigh the tax disadvantages. The corporation, and this is the salient point, applies corporate assets to the motion picture in production under the auspices of the PD agreement. That is to say, the film listed in the PD agreement is the corporation's one and only asset. In case of breach of contract, the corporation (not the producer) will be held liable only for the amount of money the motion picture in production represents. The producer's other film and personal assets are protected.

The advantages and disadvantages of this type of agreement are listed below and should be considered.

Advantages	*Disadvantages*
The producer retains day-to-day control over the project.	In case of disagreements between producer and talent, labs, production entities, and so on, the studio—since its rights are derivative—may be of little help to the producer.
The producer retains the right to contact talent and key personnel.	
The producer has somewhat more input as far as creative control is concerned.	
	Unless the studio has guaranteed the contract signed by the producer, the producer has sole responsibility.
It is not easy for the studio to move away from a project protected by the no-asset corporation.	

The producer enters into a PD agreement with the studio. If the producer is not protected by a no-asset corporation, he or she will be responsible personally for all damages that may arise during the production or in the event of breach of contract.

Advantages	*Disadvantages*
The studio is responsible for all contracts signed.	In case of takeover, it is easier for the studio to remove all personnel (including the producer) from the project. A takeover, of course, can take place under the no-asset PD agreement, as well, but then the procedure is difficult and time-consuming.
It is the studio's responsibility to intermediate if disagreements arise between producer, labs, talent, and so on.	

Advantages	*Disadvantages*
	The studio has the right to assign a studio representative to the project.
	The producer loses the day-to-day control over the film.
	The producer may lose creative control over the film.

And now I'd like to draw your attention to the fact that the discussed points are supposed to give information only. The scope of this book does not permit a discussion of legal details. And it is impossible to determine whether a producer/PD agreement or corporation/PD agreement is the most beneficial; it differs from film to film. Therefore, it is imperative that you discuss the pros and cons of each with your attorney, as well as have the PD agreement itself scrutinized closely.

Regardless of which type of setup seems best for your project, always be aware of the fact that you, one way or the other, are in the studio's employment. Therefore, make certain that you are a well-paid employee. Rather than accepting a sizable net profit participation, have your attorney negotiate a higher salary and a lower net profit participation.

Why? Aren't your pictures going to make millions?

Sure, your picture will make millions of dollars, but how much of the fortune will trickle down to you is rather dubious. So, take a deep breath before reading the next few pages, in which I'll try to shed some light on the most common studio accounting practices.

The following is a *hypothetical* cost and profit scenario for the average $20 million studio-financed distributed motion picture.

Actual production cost	$20,000,000
15% studio overhead	3,000,000
10% interest on both production cost and overhead.	2,300,000

These interest rates will run (hopefully) for about two years, if we assume one year's duration for preproduction, production, and postproduction, and another year for distribution. Make certain that interest is charged *only* from the commencement of each period, and as funds are released to you.

Print and advertising expenses to open the film amounting roughly to about half of the production cost	10,000,000
10% interest rate on costs for prints and advertising	1,000,000
So far the film has accrued a negative cost of	36,300,000
For argument's sake, let's assume the film in domestic theatrical release played in (earned).	$40,000,000

This amount does not reflect the box office receipt but the amount due to the distributor. From this amount the distributor will deduct:

40% cost for additional prints and additional advertising.	16,000,000
30% distribution fee	12,000,000

Next the film goes into overseas distribution for all areas (theatrical, TV, cable, home video)

Assuming the film plays in another	$40,000,000
35% (sometimes 40%) distribution fee	14,000,000
If a subdistributor has been employed his or her fee has to be deducted	4,000,000
10% for additional advertising overseas	4,000
10% interest rate on additional advertising	400
For auxiliary rights, such as home video, cable,	$15,000,000
network, and syndicated TV, receipts for 20 percent distribution fee	3,000,000

And finally (yes, there is no end to it) the studio takes on a 5% gross participation fee on *all* receipts. These receipts amount to the receipts received, and do not deduct expenses.

5% gross participation fee on all receipts	4,775,000
Receipts domestically	$95,000,000
Expenses:	
Prints	
Advertising	
Overhead charges	
Distribution fee	
Interest	$90,079,400

As you can tell, the profit margin is slim. If you wonder why a studio remains in business, and even prospers, remember that studios are in the distribution business. They make their living even though a film may barely break even, or might be considered a flop. For this purpose we will compare *actual* expenses with fees and interest rates.

Expenses	
Production expenses	$20,000,000
Studio overhead	3,000,000
Print and advertising expenses (to open the film)	10,000,000
Additional prints and advertising	16,000,000
Subdistributor fees overseas	4,000,000
Total expenses	$53,000,000

You see, the fairly modest budget of $20,000,000 has almost tripled by the time all expenses have been added. Now take a look at the amount of fees and interest rates the studio charges. (As far as interest rates are concerned, we must remember that the studio must pay interest, too.)

Fees and Interest Rates	
10% interest on both production cost and overhead	$ 2,300,000
10% interest rate on prints and advertising needed to open film	1,000,000
30% distribution fee domestically	12,000,000
35% distribution fee overseas	14,000,000
10% interest rate for additional overseas distribution fees	400,000
20% distribution fee for auxiliary markets	3,000,000
Total amount of fees and interest rates	$32,700,000
Plus 5% gross participation fees (based upon the entire amount of gross receipts.)	1,600,350

The Formal PD Agreement

The studio and the corporation and/or producer enter into a formal PD agreement. Most likely a studio will submit to you a lengthy (between twenty and fifty pages) standard contract, called a "boilerplate." Changes, omissions, and revisions are always negotiable. Before entering into any agreement, discuss the changes. Find out which clauses are readily changed and which ones are likely to be sticky issues. The following gives you a picture of the most important clauses of the PD agreement:

1. Contracting Control
2. Artistic Control
3. Financial Control
4. Breach of Contract
5. Takeover
6. Termination of Project
7. Over-Budget Penalty
8. Interest Charges
9. Overhead Charges
10. Insurance (liability, negative insurance, cast insurance)
11. Union Contracts
12. Producer's Warranties
13. Producer's Billing
14. Delivery of Motion Picture
15. Accounting Rights
16. Assignment of Rights
17. Producer's Payment
18. Producer's Profit Participation

Only the most basic points of each clause will be discussed. Everything mentioned has been written to give you facts, but, as mentioned before, it is your attorney's responsibility to interpret these facts and to negotiate the most favorable terms for you.

1. *Contracting Control.* Under the producer PD agreement the studio contracts creative talent and key personnel, while under the corporation PD agreement, the control remains with the producer. The studio, of course, will take an assignment of each contract, or will receive a power of attorney from the producer.

2. *Artistic Control.* Artistic control rests (depending on the contract) with either the studio or the producer. To avoid disagreement, the PD agreement should identify these controls. The fairest way to handle artistic control is to have the producer propose names but give the studio the final decision. In

practice, the convention of proposal selection applies to stars, director, art director, composer, and director of cinematography. All other assignments are usually left to the producer's discretion.

3. *Financial Control.* Since financial control is one of the most important (and most controversial) clauses of any PD agreement, the following need to be identified in unmistakable terms:

> Studio commits to finance the total cost of picture, such as production costs, prints, and advertising.

> The producer is not responsible for any production and/or distribution costs. The producer will not be liable for any over-budget costs arising from:

> Acts of God
> Defaults by third parties (actors, labs, etc.)
> Changes requested by the studio

Since you can expect arguments about this particular addition, you may sweeten the pot by providing a *completion bond.* A completion bond is a type of special insurance that guarantees additional funds in case the picture should go over budget. Since the cost of such a bond is rather high, it behooves the producer to have this amount tacked on to the production cost of the film.

The studio usually takes copyright ownership (that is to say, the studio owns the literary property, and whoever owns the literary property owns the project). In some cases (under a corporation PD agreement, for example), the studio takes a security interest in the copyright of the literary property plus the preprint material. The monies needed to produce the film are considered loans, and the studio, understandably, receives interest on them.

- The studio will require having a production account opened in a bank of its choice.
- The studio will require having a production accountant of its choice assigned to the project.
- The studio will assign one of its production executives to the picture.
- The studio reserves the right to take over the production in case of default, breach of contract, and/or over budget.

Since the studio may keep the terminology of those clauses rather loose, it is your attorney's responsibility to clarify each.

4. *Breach of Contract.* Clarify *all* conditions that may be construed as breach of contract. Most likely these will be:

- Picture went considerably over budget.
- Picture was not delivered on time.
- Picture's concept was changed *without* studio's approval.

Do *not* accept as breach of contract any damages resulting from defaults by third parties (actors, labs, locations).

5. *Takeover.* In case a studio takes over a picture, the studio has the right to remove and replace all personnel (including the producer) connected to the project. It is important to have the following provision spelled out in the PD agreement: A person can only be removed from the project if he or she has acted in an irresponsible or egregious manner (believe me, that is hard to prove).

6. *Termination of Project.* Generally a project will be terminated as a measure of last resort, and only if a production threatens to go out of control completely. Since closing a production and opening it again is costly, a studio takes this measure seriously.

7. *Over-Budget Penalty.* A picture is considered over budget if the monies spent on production exceed the approved budget. It is customary, and no studio will object, if the producer adds a 10 percent contingency for unforeseen expenditures. The following should not fall within the area of over budget:

- Unforeseen raises in guild salaries
- Additions and changes requested by the studio
- Acts of God

The producer should foresee any difficulties arising, and have the attorney ask for:

- Exclusions
- Definition of over budget and over-budget add-back penalties

Most likely the over-budget cost will be subject to interest rates:

Production	$20,000,000
Over budget	5,000,000
10% add-back penalty	500,000
10% interest	275,000

Needless to say, the studio will charge the customary interest rate of 10 percent on over-budget and add-back penalty, in which case the producer is liable to pay interest on the additional $5,500,000.

8. *Interest Charges.* A studio's interest rate exceeds the customary prime rate of 2 percent. It is important to clarify the commencement of interest payments. A studio may hold the position that interest commences as soon as the production loan has been approved, while producers contend that interest ought to be charged in concert with monies received for the production.

9. *Overhead Charges.* As discussed in our scenario, a studio charges 15 percent overhead on production expenses. You, the producer, are entitled to charge overhead (during preproduction, production, and postproduction) on the following items:

Office rental
Secretary salaries
Office supplies
Telephone
Attorney's fees

10. *Insurance.* It goes without saying that the PD agreement demands that the producer arrange for proper insurance:

1. Production liability insurance
2. Errors and omissions insurance. At times the studio will provide this type of insurance protecting the studio as well as the picture from claims such as:
   Invasion of privacy
   Libel
   Slander
   Copyright infringement

Most likely the above claims arise from material contained in the literary property. It is for this reason that if the producer deals with a controversial script and/or idea, "errors and omissions" insurance should be obtained prior to contacting a studio.

If you are shooting a scene including "civilians" (onlookers who have not been hired as extras), have every one of them sign a release form.

The errors and omissions insurance should be obtained to cover not less than $10,000,000 with a deductible of $100,000.

Raw Stock Insurance. Since suppliers of raw stock limit their liability to replacement of faulty raw stock only, raw stock insurance covers the cost of having to reshoot scenes.

Negative Insurance. This insurance protects the negative of your film against damage incurred when stored in the lab, or during transportation from studio and/or location to lab, and from the lab to editing facilities.

Miscellaneous Insurance:

Workers' Compensation
Fire, theft, property insurance
Third-party liability insurance

Cast Insurance. Most likely the studio carries an umbrella cast insurance. Again, some producers prefer to be covered by an insurance policy of their own. The cost of cast insurance depends usually on the proposed film's negative cost. The basic premium covers six people: the director and five actors. All persons covered have to submit to medical examinations by a physician appointed by the insurance company. If a person does not meet the requirements, this person may be excluded from the policy, or (more likely) a higher premium will be collected. Cast insurance comes into effect if an actor or director is injured or dies. For this reason the production company *must* sign an affidavit stating that none of the insured personnel will engage in any hazardous activities, and that for such activities stunt personnel are to be employed.

In case of an actor's death, the options are whether to replace the actor and reshoot segments of the film, or to terminate the project. Even though a producer and studio favor reshooting, the insurance company usually opts for termination of the film.

11. *Union Contracts.* The producer is responsible to enter into agreements with unions. It is interesting to note that there are no reciprocity agreements between the unions. A producer may choose to become signatory with one

but not with any other union. This does not hold true if you are producing a movie for a major studio; in this case you'll have to sign with all unions. (Yet, even if you are producing a low-budget film and have SAG actors on your casting list, you *must* sign with SAG [Screen Actors Guild]. SAG will agree to reduce scale for its members if you are producing a film budgeted under $1 million. You must, however, observe SAG regulations pertaining to overtime and meal penalties, and are to pay certain amounts to the SAG pension fund.) Also, be advised that you cannot employ SAG and nonunion actors on the same shoot. If one actor on your shoot is a member of SAG, *all* actors must be SAG members. But don't worry; if during your casting sessions you discover a terrific actor who happens to be nonunion, all it takes is a letter from you to SAG requesting to have this actor admitted to the union. Furthermore, to assure that actors will be paid the producer must deposit a bond securing actors' salaries. This bond must be deposited with SAG.

The following is a list of unions you will, or may have to, deal with:

- Screen Actors Guild (SAG)—actors
- Writers Guild of America (WGA)—writers
- Directors Guild of America (DGA)—directors, assistant directors, production managers
- Screen Extras Guild (SEG)—extras
- American Federation of Musicians (AFM)—musicians, composers, arrangers
- Theatrical Stage Employees Union (LATSE)—grips, gaffers, transportation workers
- Cinematographers Union—cinematographers, camera operators, loaders

12. *Producer's Warranties.* The studio will require the producer to submit what is called a "chain of documents" regarding the literary property. This chain refers to the documents the producer has previously obtained from the copyright holder of the literary property. In addition, the following documents have to be submitted:

- An errors and omissions insurance policy (in case the studio does not carry one).
- Agreement that the producer will refrain from placing a lien on the project.

- The producer indemnification against any claim arising from breach of contract by third parties.
- Agreement by the producer not to obtain a loan based upon expected net profits.
- Agreement by the producer not to assign any sum due him or her to any third party.

It is obvious that the producer has no remedies against the studio. In case of alleged breach of contract, the producer can sue for monetary damage only, and cannot keep the studio from distributing and/or merchandising the picture.

13. *Producer's Billing.* The typical standard or boilerplate contract contains several clauses regarding the producer's billing.

The producer's screen credits have to be positioned on a single title card, and must roll before the director's credit on front titles.

The producer's credit has to appear in proper size on one-sheets, and *all* newspaper advertising.

The producer has the right to supply the studio with billing requirements.

Laboratory Pledge-holder Agreement. The studio customarily will use in-house lab and editing facilities, or will assign a lab of its choice to the production. In the event the producer has been permitted to employ a lab of his or her choice, the studio retains the legal title to the motion picture via a "laboratory pledge-holder agreement," guaranteeing that only the studio will have access to the negative.

14. *Delivery of Motion Picture.* The studio reserves the right to the final cut of the picture. The items to be delivered are discussed in detail in the Distribution Agreement on pages 90–91.

15. *Accounting Rights.* Most PD agreements provide for quarterly accountings during the film's first two-year run. After this time period the producer receives semiannual and finally annual accountings.

16. *Assignment of Rights.* In the event the producer elects to dispose his or her net profits, the producer agrees to offer these to the studio first.

17. *Producer's Payment.* Once a studio has accepted a project for development, the studio will have to pay the producer a nominal fee (about $25,000) plus compensation of all expenses incurred in the project so far. If the project goes into "turnabout," that is to say, if the studio has lost interest in the project, the producer is entitled to a small compensation, usually not exceeding $30,000.

Once the studio has approved your production, you should negotiate for a set payment schedule:

10% of the producer's compensation in biweekly installments during the preproduction period

50% of compensation in weekly installments during the production period

10% of compensation at delivery of picture

or:

1/3 of compensation at the commencement of preproduction

1/3 of compensation at commencement of production

1/3 of compensation upon delivery of picture

18. *Producer's Profit Participation.* At times, the producer's profit participation gives rise to heated negotiations. (We will discuss gross and net profit in detail a little later.) Suffice it to say that if you have any doubts about the studio's accounting, you have the right to audit the studio's books. Such an audit is expensive, and the results are doubtful. In any event, you have the right to audit receipts and expenses applying to *your film only.* For this reason the following information, pertinent to your audit, is difficult if not impossible to obtain:

Was the film used to cross-collaborate a less successful picture? There is always the possibility that the loss on one film has been offset with the gross profits of another film as far as distribution expenses and advertising are concerned.

Yet you should have no difficulty obtaining the following information:

1. Has my film been given sufficient play dates?
2. Was enough money spent on prints and advertising?

The "Pick-Up" Deal: The Producer's Distribution Agreement with a Studio

The distribution agreement comes into play when the studio agrees to distribute a picture that has either already been financed, or has been completed, especially for foreign distribution.

The financial scenario, except for the amount spent to produce a film, is the same as for the studio-produced-and-distributed motion picture.

The distribution contract, however, differs greatly. Again, as in the PD agreement, do not tackle the distribution agreement by yourself, but enlist the help of an attorney and an accountant. Even though most distribution agreements are standard boilerplate, they contain many clauses requiring negotiation and/or clarification. The following is an example of a distribution agreement:

1. Date
2. Picture
3. Elements: Producer
   Director
   Screenplay written by
   Screenplay based upon the following literary property
   Stars
   Running time
   Production year and rating
4. Budget
5. Production company (called grantor)
6. Distribution company (called grantee)
7. Delivery date
8. Distribution period (usually perpetuity)
9. Territories: listing territories (usually universe)
10. Rights granted:
    Producer grants the distribution company all rights to the
      picture, including the copyright.
    Distributor has the right to distribute the picture (listing medias).
    Distributor has the right to music publishing and merchandising.
    Distributor has the right to all underlying rights in and to the
      picture.
    (Note: Make certain that *all* rights are spelled out.)

11. Gross Receipts:

    Determines the accounting of gross receipts. (Note: Gross receipts ought to include *all* monies received and/or credited from all media.)

12. Net Receipts:

    Determines the amount to be paid to the production company.

    Determines the way distribution fees and distribution expenses are to be deducted from the gross receipts.

    Determines that all third-party profit participation has to be deducted from the producer's profits.

    Determines the producer's participation in net profits.

13. Accounting:

    Determines the producer's right to audit books.

    Determines the distributor's accounting period, usually quarterly and delivered sixty to ninety days after the reporting period. (Note: Try to negotiate for a sixty-day period.)

14. Advance and/or Minimum Guarantee:

    Determines whether or not the distributor will give an advance or minimum guarantee. (Most likely a distribution will grant neither to the first-time producer.)

15. Distribution Expenses:

    Determines the distribution expenses.

16. Distribution fees:

    Determines the percentage the distributor collects from the gross receipts; usually between 30 and 40%:

- Domestic theatrical
- Cable
- Network television
- Syndicated television
- Theatrical, television, home video—overseas

    Determines the percentage of the royalties the distributor receives from domestic home video sales.

    Determines the agent's fee (if an agent was involved in any of the above transactions. The agent's fee should not be higher than 10%).

17. Delivery of specific items:

    Film:

        Original negative

Optical soundtrack negative
Three-track magnetic master of the soundtrack
Answer print
Color-corrected interpositive
Titles
Titleless background
Separate soundtracks: dialog track
                               sound-effects track
                               music track
M&E track
Outtakes and trims
Television cover shots

Video:

Digital video master: one in NTS format
                           one in PAL format*
Digital television master: one in NTS format
                                     one in PAL format
Digital trailers: one in NTS format
                  one in PAL format

Trailer:

Picture negative
Optical soundtrack negative
Magnetic soundtrack negative
Answer print
Textless background
Soundtrack

18. Publicity: Producer grants distributor the right to promote and advertise the picture.

    The producer has to submit the following materials:
        Stills and negatives: black-and-white and color.
        Color slides
        Electronic press kit

19. Aspect ratio: Standard theatrical 1:85 to 1

20. Rating: Distributor has the right to submit picture to the MPAA for rating. Rating fee has to be paid by producer.

21. Artwork: Distributor is responsible for the creation of artwork.

---

*Overseas studios demand PAL formats.

22. Editing: Distributor reserves the right to reedit the picture.
23. Dailies: Distributor reserves the right to view dailies.
24. Warranties: Producer warrants to keep distributor free of all liens and claims.

   Producer warrants that there are no claims, legal actions, or suits against the picture or the company.

   Producer warrants that all third-party participations have been disclosed.

   Producer warrants that he or she has the right to enter into said agreement.

25. Security interest: Distributor will be granted security interest in the picture. (Note: This clause should be omitted unless distributor has given an advance or participates in financing the picture.)
26. Termination
27. Indemnities:

   Producer shall hold distributor and its subsidiaries, distributors, officers, and representatives harmless from all obligations arising from claims, damages, etc.

   Distributor grants identical warranties to producer.

28. Residuals: Producer shall be liable to pay residuals.
29. Act of God (Force Majeure):

   Distributor has the right to discontinue marketing picture in case of acts of God.

30. Documents: Producer has to deliver the following documents to distributor:

   Laboratory access letter
   Sound laboratory access letter
   Original screenplay
   Script supervisor's notes
   Dialog spotting list
   Synopsis of screenplay
   Music cue sheets
   Credit list, and screen credit obligation list
   Talent agreements

31. Legal documents: Producer has to deliver the following documents to distributor:

   • Copyright certificates (U.S. copyright registration certificates issued by the Library of Congress)

- Copyright report
- Notarized assignment of rights
- Music licenses

32. Errors and Omissions Insurance: Producer shall furnish distributor with a copy of errors and omissions insurance.
33. Conditions Precedent: This clause lists conditions, if not met, rendering the contract null and void. (Note: Have your attorney negotiate each and every clause listed.)
34. Governing Law: This clause deals with arbitration and/or legal actions in case of disagreements.
35. Signatures: The standard distribution agreement has many points in common with the PD agreement. Do not sign on the dotted line until your attorney and accountant have scrutinized the document carefully.

> The average distribution agreement runs between twenty-five and thirty-five pages. A volume of fifty pages is not unheard of. Each and every clause warrants your attention and has to be dealt with thoroughly.
>
> Have your attorney negotiate terms that are either vague or seemingly unfavorable for you. Discuss financing clauses and distributor's demands with your accountant.
>
> And always remember, distributors do not grant you a favor by taking on your film. They need films to stay in business.

Mini-Majors

Mini-majors are powerful companies that operate very much like the major studios. They finance and distribute pictures of high artistic quality and strong audience appeal, and at times pick up a film here and there. In order to gain access to the more lucrative domestic and foreign markets, they distribute their products through the major studios.

Unfortunately, mini-majors do not weather economic changes as well as the majors do, and a company that did fantastically initially might be out of business after a few years. How come? Well, in today's world, major studios are but divisions of huge corporations. Losses sustained by the film division of a conglomerate are easily, and at times gladly, absorbed by the parent corporation.

Mini-majors do not enjoy the financial umbrella of their major studio counterparts. A number of unsuccessful films can wipe out a company.

The advice given about PD agreements and distribution agreements in the section on major studios applies to the mini-majors as well.

5.

Other distributors,

other deals

And now let's take a look at the independent distributor. The success of your film depends on its successful distribution. The right independent distributor can make a small film "take off," while another, seemingly equally well qualified independent keeps your film toddling along on the road to oblivion. Therefore, take time before you approach any distributor. Find out about the distributor as much as you possibly can. While it is difficult to ascertain an independent distributor's financial strength, you'll find out easily enough:

Does the distributor handle your film's genre?

Does the distributor handle films that are budget-wise similar to your film?

What is the distributor's main area of concentration?
  Domestic distribution
  Foreign distribution
  Home video
  Cable

Once you have decided upon an independent, you'll have to think about the correct approach. Admittedly, you are in a better and far stronger position if you approach an independent after your film has been completed. (Yet, as things stand at the time of writing of this book you do need a distributor's letter of intent, or at least a letter of interest, to obtain financing.) On the other hand, if you approach the distributor after your picture has been completed, you are missing out on highly important and helpful input. The distributor knows what sells, and usually will be able to sense what might be selling a year from now, when your picture is completed. For this reason the distributor's input, as far as story line, stars, and director are concerned, can be invaluable.

But you also have to be very careful not to sacrifice your prospective film's theme and visualized mood. Always be wary that the distributor might try to fit your prospective movie within the framework of all the films he or she distributes generally.

Probably the most unsatisfactory approach is to film a demo tape for prospective distributors. I am amazed how many beginning producers still believe in this method, and how much time and, even more important, money they waste by pursuing this ill-fated approach.

Remember, a demo tape *never* shows what the finished film will be like. No distributor can decide upon acceptance or rejection of your film on a five- or ten-minute demo reel.

And this brings us to the sad truth that producers often tend to view distributors—whether major studio, mini-major, or independent—as money-grabbing machines. True, it seems unreasonable for distributors to charge interest rates, take their fees off the top of box office or foreign receipts, and disregard the producer's responsibility of paying back bank loans and bank interest charges and/or partner investments. But remember the enormous overhead majors have to absorb by maintaining costly studios and an extensive national and international distribution network. Independents, on the other hand, while not faced with these expenses, do advance—as do the majors and mini-majors—extensive sums for prints and advertising as well as to foreign sales agents. (We will discuss domestic and foreign distribution next.)

So why not forget about the distributor as the ogre, and instead look at the distributor as the producer's partner. Don't ever forget, the distributor needs you, the producer, to supply the product, and you need the distributor to get the film to the people; it is as simple as that. Granted, the distributor has not chosen this line of work for purely altruistic reasons; the distributor is in it to make money and so are you: Don't ever lose sight of that.

Consequently, don't approach any distributor with naive trust or antagonistic wariness, but from the very beginning of your negotiations look upon him or her as your partner. This approach, however, should not keep you from being concerned about your own interest, that is to say, evaluate each and every clause in your distribution contract carefully, and have your attorney and accountant negotiate unsatisfactory points, as well as clarify the opaque ones. It is true, such negotiations might lead to heated arguments, but it is far better to straighten things out in the beginning of a relationship (the producer-distributor relationship is a close one) than to stew, pout, argue, and possibly litigate later on. It is equally true that bringing forth your demands might cause the distributor to lose interest in your project. And this is just as well, because this particular distributor would have been wrong for you anyway.

As you and your attorney look at your prospective distributor's distribution contract, keep in mind that this contract—the same as the major studio's PD agreement—is heavily loaded in favor of the distributor. Still, after you have made your demands known, there is no reason why distributor and producer should not work together amiably. (By the way, the independent distributor's contract is almost identical to the one favored by the majors and mini-majors we discussed in the last chapter.) Make certain that the contract contains the following provisions:

- The amount spent on P&A *must* be specified (never forget that you the producer have to pay for these expenses later on).
- Have recoupment and gross profit defined in clear terms.
- Clarify whether any interest rates will be charged on the P&A expenses (most likely interest will be charged).
- Clarify whether or not exhibitors will participate in advertising expenses. Find out about the percentage rate of participation.
- Set a ceiling for both prints and advertising expenses.
- Determine which amount is considered the base for the distributor's 30% distribution fee:
  - Box office receipts
  - The distributor's share of box office receipts

A few years ago independents paid a sizable advance to the producer, and even gave negative pick-up deals. Those times have passed, and I doubt whether they will ever return. Independent distributors now refrain from even giving a minimum guarantee.

It is no secret that independent distributors face certain difficulties in obtaining theaters *and* collecting money from the exhibitors, both resulting in reduced box office receipts. Independents distribute relatively few pictures a year and have less leverage with exhibitors; they therefore see their films booked into less desirable theaters, theaters that show rather small box office receipts. Still, distributing your film through an experienced independent gives your product an excellent chance for not only recouping the investor's money but making a small profit as well.

After this lengthy but necessary introduction, let's take a careful look at the independent's areas of distribution: domestic distribution and foreign distribution.

Domestic Distribution. Domestic distribution refers to domestic playdates within the United States and Canada. While the major studios operate their own domestic and foreign distribution facilities and are dealing with major theater chains only, the independent has to rely upon domestic territorial subdistributors. Territorial subdistributors, also called territorials, may represent one territory, or they may work in several areas. A California-based territorial may supply exhibitors in California, Arizona, and Nevada.

Usually distributor and subdistributor share advertising expenses (they do not share cost of prints). This cost sharing is called "cooperative advertising." The exhibitor usually takes 20 percent "off the floor," that is to say, 20 percent off the box office receipts. The remainder will be shared according to the exhibitor's share of advertising payments; for example, exhibitor/distributor participation may be 20/80, 30/70, 40/60* or—the most common —50/50.

At this time it might be a good idea to dispel some of the box office myths. Agreed, we read about box office receipts ranging in the tens of millions. A $50-, $75-, or even $90-million domestic box office is not unheard of. But remember: Only majors take in such fantastic amounts of money; these box office receipts apply to blockbuster Christmas and summer releases; and, most important, the studios receive only about half of the box office intake.

To get an accurate picture of an independent's "strength," you must ask these questions:

- Will my film be distributed in the off-seasons (April–June, August–November)? Your film has a much better chance to succeed if exhibited in the off-seasons.

---

*40% to the exhibitor, 60% to the distributor.

- What specific areas will be targeted for distribution of my film? If your film is an action and/or horror film you are far better off if it is exhibited in areas not favored with major studios' second-string films.
- How many prints will be cut? It is more advantageous to the producer if a smaller number of prints (about 200 to 500) make the rounds.
- What is the extent of advertising? (Look at the media list. Ask for tear sheets of ads.)
- Will I receive copies of the distribution schedule and box office receipts?
- Will the distributor handle the auxiliary markets of home video, cable, network, and syndicated television?

The following is a hypothetical scenario illuminating the domestic release picture, including the auxiliary market:

Production cost of film	$ 2,500,000

(We assume that the film was financed by partnership investment, and therefore no interest rates are to be considered.)

Distribution expenses	
500 prints at $1,500	$ 750,000
10% interest rate	75,000
Advertising expenses	1,000,000
if shared 50/50, with territorial advertising cost	500,000
charged to producer	
10% on advertising cost	50,000
Total distribution costs:	$ 2,375,000
Box office receipts	$10,000,000

Fees to be deducted from box office receipts
20% off the floor to exhibitor $ 2,000,000
Participation in box office receipts
50/50 share of remaining box office receipts. After the
exhibitor's off-the-floor fee has been deducted the
distributor will take in $4,000,000.

Amounts to be deducted from gross box office receipts of	$ 4,000,000
Cost for prints	750,000
Interest rate	75,000
Advertising expenses (distributor's share)	500,000
10% interest rate	50,000
30% distribution cost on distributor's take of $4,000,000	$ 1,200,000
Total amount to be paid by producer	$ 2,500,000
Income from auxiliary markets	
Cable sales	$ 2,000,000
Home video sales	1,540,000
Network and syndicated sales	500,000
Total amount of auxiliary sales	4,000,000
If your distributor handles these sales a fee of 20% will be deducted	808,000
Amount due to producer	$ 3,232,000

The above scenario assumes that the exhibitors do pay the amounts due to the distributor, and that both exhibitors and distributor pay promptly.

And now a few words about auxiliary sales:

Since home video (theatrical and instructional) has become such a vital part of today's distribution picture, an entire chapter has been devoted to it. (Presently, we will examine cable and TV sales.) First, a producer does not necessarily need a distributor to arrange auxiliary sales. A savvy producer can easily manage these sales. Nevertheless, if your film is on the upper scale— say, between $2,500,000 and $5,000,000—it is probably more advantageous to have your distributor handle the auxiliary sales. In fact, most medium-sized independents insist upon handling auxiliary rights.

About auxiliary rights the producer has to know that:

- There is a window (a certain, negotiated time period) between your film's theatrical exhibit and its cable exposure.
- Most likely cable will either give the producer an advance, or buy (negative pick-up) the film outright.
- Advances and negative payments are usually stretched out over one year. You'll receive your payment in four equal installments.
- A $5,000,000 film may bring in about $2,500,000 to $4,000,000.

- There is another window of about six months to one year between cable and home video exhibit of your film.
- The advance for a film depends on how successful a film has been theatrically. And this is the reason, as mentioned previously, that a domestic theatrical release is imperative for any producer. Most likely your advance for a $5,000,000 film will run between $750,000 and $1,000,000.
- You may expect about 200,000 tapes to hit the video stores. If the tape sells for $30 wholesale, you may expect the following scenario:

*Wholesale price of one unit (tape)**	$30
60% discount (combined discount for wholesaler and retailer) per unit =	$18
25% to manufacturer (if tape is not being made by major studio) Percentage to be deducted from wholesale price of $30	$ 7.50
From the adjusted gross profit per unit of $4.50, the distributor deducts 20%.	$ 0.90
This brings the producer's net profit to	$ 3.60

Considering that 200,000 tapes have been distributed to retailers, you may expect a windfall of about $720,000.

A net profit of $720,000 is nothing to be brushed off if, and that is the point, *if* all your tapes sell. All manufacturers permit retailers to rerun tapes, and most likely between 30 and 50 percent of the tapes will be returned, to be sold for a discount later on.

After a certain time period (window), network TV, and later on syndication, will show your film. Usually some income trickles in for about five years.

Since your film is in a package with a great number of other films, it is difficult to ascertain the amount of money the producer will actually receive. Also, remember that the *producer*, not the exhibitor, is responsible for the

---

*The following scenario pertains to theatrical videos only, and does not apply to instructional tapes.

residuals because of actors appearing in the films. But take heart; you, the producer, do not have to employ a full-time bookkeeper; SAG keeps track of residual payments due their members.

Foreign Distribution. Some independents distribute domestically as well as overseas. Most of them work together with agents specializing in overseas sales. (If, however, you have a distribution agreement with a mini-major, don't fail to have your attorney add the following clause to the distribution contract: "The United Kingdom, Australia, France, Germany, Italy, Spain and Japan *will not* be licensed on an outright sales basis." The other territories, of course, will be sold on an outright basis, that is, for a fixed sum.

The independent distributor who handles foreign sales does not have the sales access the majors and mini-majors enjoy, and does not deal with the buyers purchasing films for important territories. As the independent deals with a number of small territories only, it is far better to accept a fixed sum that includes theatrical as well as home-video and possibly cable and TV.

Your film will be sold at all film markets. These, I can assure you, are not the glamorous affairs as pictured in glitzy novels and entertaining films and TV shows. These so-called festivals are hard-nosed sales conventions. Here is how they operate: Several hotels are taken over by the sellers. Majors and mini-majors occupy entire floors (they are the ones who throw elaborate parties); the run-of-the-mill seller rents a room in one of the big hotels. This room plays host to a number of TV sets, one next to the other, all showing the distributor's films over and over. Buyers walk from room to room, take a short look at the displayed wares, take the sell sheets the distributor hands out, and if interested return to watch one of the tapes.

But let's go back to the film markets. First of all, do not confuse them with the many, many film festivals that are held all over the United States and Europe. Film festivals are concerned with a film's artistic merit; film markets are concerned with a film's monetary prospects. While some films made their way from festivals to the film markets, most fail to do so. These are the film markets where your film, you hope, will be shown and sold:

Cannes Film Festival   Cannes, France—April
This festival has been geared primarily to the requirements of majors and mini-majors. Cannes may show some profitable sales for the medium-sized independent, but this market is a waste of time and money for the small-time distributor.

MIFED   Milan, Italy—October
This is the most lucrative market for the distributor of low-budget
films.

Los Angeles Film Market   Los Angeles, California—February
Somewhat in between Cannes and Milan, as far as importance is
concerned. The Los Angeles Film Market attracts new majors as well
as the small distributors and buyers.

Foreign sales are complicated at best, and no producer should even think
about selling films at one of the film markets without help. Each territory
(country) has different import and tax regulations that must be met. The
smaller independent distributor works with a number of sales agents, all well
versed about the regulations, taxes, and customs of their respective territories.
Film markets are expensive. The independent distributors charge:

40% distribution fee
10% foreign agent's fee or 20% subdistribution fee

Expenses include advertising and film market overhead (such as distribution booth rental, hotel, flight, meals, and entertainment). You see,
expenses encompass a wide area, and it is for this reason that the producer
ought to set a ceiling on distribution expenses.

At times, an independent distributor prefers to work with a foreign subdistributor instead of an agent. If your film is technically and artistically well
done, you have a good chance that the subdistributor will pay an advance
against the independent distributor's expected gross receipts. The subdistributor keeps all gross receipts until the advance and the 20 percent distribution
fee have been recouped.

The money the distributor receives is called an "overage." From this
amount the independent distributor draws between 30 and 35 percent distribution fee. If the distributor works with an agent instead of a subdistributor,
the distribution fee ranges between 35 and 40 percent.

Unfortunately, monies earned through foreign sales are not as readily
available as you might wish. Here's the typical chain of events:

1. The foreign buyer sends a letter of credit (LC) to the foreign
   distributor, who in turn submits the LC to your U.S. distributor.

2. Sometimes the LC has a due time of several months (and you hope that the LC won't be canceled).
3. Not until the LC comes due, and has been cashed, are you expected to submit the following items to the foreign buyer:
   Negative copy of the film
   Optical soundtrack
   Dialog track
   Sound effects track
   Music track (if requested, and paid for by foreign buyer, the producer has to submit a foreign dialog track)
   Titles
   Textless background (for titles)
   M-E track (magnetic soundtrack)
   Cover shots for television
   Digital video master
   Digital TV master
   Trailer
   Black-and-white stills
   Color slides
   Advertising material (artwork for one-sheets and mats)
   Script (English version)
   Production book (copy of script supervisor's notes)
   Cover shots (some foreign countries rightfully are opposed to violence, and more palatable scenes have to be submitted. It is a good idea to include these cover shots in your production schedule)

As you can tell, the materials to be submitted are plentiful and costly. And, yes, it is the producer's responsibility to pay for them.

This is a foreign sales scenario:

Income from 10 territories	$10,000,000
Expenses	
20% distribution fee for foreign distributor	$ 2,000,000
35% for independent distributor	3,500,000
Distribution expenses	500,000
Materials submitted to foreign buyers (If possible, the producer should pay for the material expenses,	50,000

because if the distributor advances the needed
amounts, the producer will have to pay a 10%
interest rate. If you have an acceptable credit rating,
labs manufacturing these materials will defer.)

Total expenses $ 6,050,000

Total due producer $ 3,950,000

Again, a word of warning: while your first year of foreign sales is the
strongest and most lucrative, do not expect to sell all territories. Looking at
the scenarios, both domestic and foreign, you'll notice the producer's net
profit—after production costs have been recouped—amounts to about
$800,000. If shared 50/50 with the investors, the producer takes home
$400,000. The investor's percentage return amounts to less than 10 percent.

And now another important point. All scenarios given in this chapter are
purely hypothetical. One can estimate the cost of a film, but no one can ever
predict domestic box office receipts and foreign sales. The given amounts are
examples and should not be used to predict a film's box office draw. Your
movie might take in more money, or it might be a loss. No one knows.

Distributor for Hire

Let's assume you have produced a small, low-budget film, and your production costs were not above $500,000. The film, shot on 35mm, is of good
technical quality, and you even have a secondary but acceptable star on your
cast list. Needless to say, you won't ever think of approaching a major or
mini-major with your project; even a run-of-the-mill independent distributor
will decline to distribute your film.

Granted, compared with the previously discussed budgets, a budget of
$500,000 seems to be a meager one. Yet the innovative producer (who most
likely is also the screenwriter and possibly director) will be able to pull it off
if he or she is a professional who knows the craft of filmmaking.

To produce a salable film on a tiny budget, be fully aware of the following:

Your film won't be accepted by an independent distributor.
Your film won't find an extensive domestic distribution.
Your film's primary profit areas are:

Domestic (U.S., Canada): home video
Foreign: all areas

Your film, even though it has been shot for home video, needs domestic distribution. The problem is that no independent distributor will handle it. What you need is the "distributor for hire." A number of highly skilled and very reputable companies specialize in your kind of film. Aware of the fact that your film's domestic distribution is a lost cause financially, they charge about $100,000 for their services. In addition, you have to supply them with:

25 release prints
One-sheets
Newspaper advertising mats

To be sure, you'll have to pay for prints and advertising materials. Conservatively speaking, you'll have to add $150,000 to $200,000 to your production budget for advertising purposes.

Give your distributor about six months to "bicycle" your film around the country. Don't dream to see your film exhibited in major cities or main multiplexes. Your film in "multiples of three or four" finds its niche in obscure areas in small, privately owned theaters. The distributor for hire pays a nominal amount to the exhibitor. In addition, the exhibitor retains all box office receipts. You don't see a penny of the box office receipts, but your film proves its all-important domestic release.

In some instances the distributor for hire four-walls your picture. This practice usually applies to theaters that show higher box office intakes than the tiny mom-and-pop theaters.

If you, the producer, have but a few prints (three to five) at your disposal and if your budget in all honesty cannot carry the services of a distributor for hire, you should try to do some four-walling yourself.

Granted, four-walling involves legwork and your film won't have the exposure of a film handled by the distributor for hire, but you'll save money.

Foreign Distribution. Let me advise you not to attend any foreign markets. First of all, booth rental is exorbitantly expensive, even if you were to partner with a number of small-time producers. And without a booth, there are no sales possibilities. You do far better by entrusting your film to one of the many experienced but small foreign distributors. You'll find their names and addresses in the film market issues of *Variety* and *Hollywood Reporter*. (The film

market issues are published about fourteen days prior to each respective market.) Approach a small foreign distributor who handles but a handful of films.
Don't expect to sell your film to any lucrative foreign territories. Your markets
are the small territories in Southeast Asia, South and Central America, and
Africa, plus a few European territories. You'll have to supply your distributor
with:

One-sheets
Sell sheets (flyers to be handed out)

As with his or her bigger counterpart, your foreign distributor will charge
distribution expenses (make certain to set a ceiling) and a distribution fee that
ranges between 35 and 40 percent. The rights to your film will be sold primarily for theatrical and home video release, even though your contract reads
"all areas." It is because of the foreign theatrical market that you *must* (forget
what some people say) shoot your film on 35mm. A film shot on 16mm
simply won't do.

Don't be disappointed if your film sells to but a few territories its first
year out. Your small, low-budget film, after all, has a foreign sales life of about
three years. Payments come slowly, but regularly.

Home Video. Just because your film is on the bottom rung of the distribution ladder, don't hesitate to approach the big home video distributors first,
then make your way down to the medium-sized ones. Have confidence in
your film, and don't hesitate to ask for an advance. The usual advance is
between $300,000 and $400,000 (yes, in this area your film compares favor-
ably with its higher-budgeted counterpart). If your film should turn out to
have legs, and sells units exceeding the recouped advance, you are entitled
to a 20 percent royalty of the tape's wholesale price.

If the distribution company does not pay an advance, you are entitled
to a 25 percent royalty off the wholesale price of each unit sold. Agreed, you
will never really know how many units have been sold, but you have to rely
upon your distributor's honesty and desire to distribute your future films.

You do not require either an agent or a distributor to contact prospective
home video distributors, but you yourself should approach each firm's director of acquisition.

Again, you'll find the names of home video distributors in the film market
issues of *Variety,* 1400 N. Cahuenga Boulevard, Los Angeles, CA 90028, and
Hollywood Reporter, 6715 Sunset Boulevard, Hollywood, CA 90028.

And now a word about home video distributors. Except for the home video departments of the major studios, the home video field is a highly fluctuating one. A distribution company may open today only to be gone tomorrow. Find out about the company you intend to do business with. Grit your teeth, pay an entertainment attorney, and find out:

How long has the distributor been in business?
Is the distributor known to be reliable?
Does the distributor advertise his products sufficiently?
Is the distributor known to pay promptly?

Cable and TV. Your chances of getting your film into cable distribution are small. In comparison, you have a good chance to have your film picked up for a *syndicated* TV package. But the revenue is small and trickles in over about five years. And even the small, low-budget producer has to pay residuals to the actors.

This is the expense/income scenario for a small, low-budget film:

Expenses	Production expenses	$600,000
	Prints and advertising	50,000
	Distributor for hire	100,000
Income	Advance home video (since you arranged the sale yourself, no distributor's percentage is due)	300,000
	Syndicated TV sale	100,000
	20% agent's fee	20,000
	Foreign sales (10 sales @ $100,000)	1,000,000
	40% Foreign distributor fee*	400,000
	Distribution expenses	50,000
	Materials submitted at $5,000 per film	50,000

*The higher percentage on the distributor's fee reflects the fact that usually no agents are involved in the sales.

Total Expenses	Production expenses	600,000
	Prints and advertising	50,000
	Distributor for hire	100,000
	Agent's fee, syndicated TV sales 20%	20,000
	Foreign sales distributor's fee 40%	400,000
	Distribution expenses	50,000
	Materials submitted	50,000
Total Incomes	Home video advance	300,000
	Syndicated TV sales	100,000
	Foreign sales	1,000,000
	Total income	$1,400,000
	Total expenses	$1,270,000
	Profit	$ 130,000

As you can tell, in terms of income your small, low-budget film compares nicely with its high-budget counterpart. But, and this is a point I wish to stress, an income scenario comparable to the one given occurs *only if your film is of excellent technical and artistic quality.* Your film must *look* like it cost about $2 million. Home video is a highly competitive business. No distributor wastes time on a mediocre film. Here are a few pointers:

Interesting, *professionally* written script
Promotional hook
Recognizable star
Professional screen actors (stage actors won't do)
Experienced key personnel
Good-quality services (labs, etc.)

Experience counts if one produces a small, low-budget film.

6.

*A*ll about profits,

gross and net

n any business, except the motion picture industry, *gross profit* (receipt) refers to income received, but *no* deduction taken; *net profit* refers to income received *after* expenses have been deducted; and *break even* has been achieved when income *equals* expenses.

Unfortunately for films, such simple equations do not hold true. The interpretation of gross, net, and break even changes from distributor to distributor, and at times it even changes from movie to movie. Since these terms are endowed with such dangerous elasticity, it behooves the producer to have them not only defined but also to have the definition spelled out in the PD agreement and/or distribution contract.

Since so much confusion arises because of the terms, and so much disagreement is inherent in them, let's take a close look at:

Gross profit (receipt)
Break even
Net profit

Gross Profit

The following is a breakdown of domestic gross profit participation.

Box office receipt deductions:

Exhibitor's "floor," the exhibitor's expenses for rent, upkeep, overhead, and salaries.

Exhibitor's advertising expenses

The remaining gross profit will be shared by distributor and exhibitor depending on the percentage of the exhibitor's promotional participation. The usual split is 50/50.

From the remaining gross profit the *distributor* deducts distribution expenses:

Distributor's advertising expenses (eventually the producer reimburses the distributor):
Taxes

Prints (another expense the producer has to carry eventually)

Overhead

Shipping charges*

The savvy producer ought to be well aware of the following distribution practice: Since the distributor receives distribution fees from the gross, the distributor gains income by keeping the gross as high as possible by postponing payment of distribution expenses as long as possible.

That practice obviously yields a higher income for the distributor, and to avoid this pitfall your attorney should add a clause stating that for the purpose of calculating participation, gross receipts received should be changed to "adjusted gross receipts," a sum that is considerably smaller, since distribution expenses have been deducted. In this scenario, the producer shares in adjusted gross once the film reaches the break-even point. If the

---

*For foreign distribution these costs will be added: collection conversion, transfer, licenses, export fees.

distributor—and watch out for this loophole—incurs additional distribution expenses, the distributor will recoup these costs before the producer can claim profit participation. Therefore, the producer must have his or her attorney add a clause to the contract, setting a ceiling on distribution expenses, that is to say:

Distribution expenses have to be kept within a certain negotiated amount.

The distributor needs the producer's *written* approval if distribution expenses are to be increased.

The producer who has to deal with third-party participation—the investors who'll recoup their investment plus percentage or profit participation; the writer, actor, director whose contracts stipulated points—faces deductions of his or her own.

From gross profits received from all sources (domestic and foreign, all area distribution) the *producer* will further deduct:

Taxes
Deferments
Interest rates (if bank loans were used)
Bank payments
Distribution expenses
Distribution fees

Break Even

Break even is the point when expenses equal income. Clearly, then, if expenses and income can be balanced no gross profit has been reached. Some distributors keep this balance by favoring a "rolling break even," which means they add new distribution expenses whenever a break even threatens. Therefore, to safeguard against such practice, the producer ought to insist that the two clauses discussed in the previous segment (distribution ceiling and producer's approval if expenses have to be increased) are contractually defined and added.

Another device that keeps a film from reaching a break even is called "cross-collateralization." The distributor offsets the income of a number of films with their respective expenses. For instance: If film I produced by producer A earns a gross receipt of $1,000, and film II produced by producer B loses $1,000, film B's loss is deducted from film A's gross receipt; in other words, both films are "cross-collateralized."

Such collateralization, no doubt, is unfair to the producer. On the other hand, if the distributor collateralizes the profits your film achieved in one area—cable, for instance—with the losses suffered in another area such as domestic distribution, collateralization is most acceptable.

So, whenever the question of cross-collateralization comes up, have your attorney make certain (and state it in the contract) that your film cannot be collateralized with any of the distributor's other films.

Net Profits. There is no standard net deal. Remember this before you, your attorney, and your accountant head for the distributor's office. And also remember that most distributors will try to convince you to settle for a 100 percent* net deal. This particular deal permits the distributor to recoup all expenses and to collect all fees before the producer sees any money. This, in my opinion, is an unfair situation. Let's not forget that the producer has the responsibility to recoup the investors' investments, and—it's hoped—pay them a little profit, while struggling to pay off a high-interest bank loan. While it is true that the fair "first-dollar gross"† deal is all but extinct, you should never agree to the 100 percent net deal. Instead you may consider (and fight hard and long for) one of the following net profit participation arrangements:

1. The distributor takes all expenses off the top and splits the remainder 50/50 with the producer. The distributor's split is considered part of the distribution fee.

Advantages
A fair deal if you know the distributor is a reliable one, and have worked with him or her previously.

Disadvantages
Risky if the distributor is an unknown entity, as the danger of a rolling break even lurks.

---

*Yes, the producer receives 100 percent of the net, but *after* the distributor has recouped distribution expenses and the distribution fee.
†The producer receives 30 percent of the distributor's gross until a negotiable point of expenditures has been reached.

2. If the producer participates in advertising expenses (but not expenses for the prints), the distributor/producer split should be 40/60. The distributor recoups expenses for prints. The distributor's split is considered part of the distribution fee.

Advantages	*Disadvantages*
10% higher profit participation.	For a mere 10% higher profit participation, the producer is stuck with part of the advertising cost.

3. If the producer participates in prints and advertising expenses, the distributor/producer split is 30/70. Distributor split is considered part of the distribution fee.

Advantages	*Disadvantages*
The producer has control over all expenses. Fraudulent distribution practices are unlikely.	Depending on your movie's scope, the monetary outlay may be excessive.

And last but not least, a few words of warning:

- Do not agree to anything and do not sign anything without your attorney's and/or accountant's advice.
- Demand straightforward answers to your questions.
- Insist that all clauses pertaining to gross and net are spelled out, and are clear and short.
- Have all distribution expenses listed in detail.

7.

Contracts:

five important contracts

every producer must

negotiate carefully

No book on the business of making a movie is complete without some advice about contracts. There are a host of contracts to be considered. Some contracts, being mostly standard boilerplate (crew, key personnel, day player), have little if any impact on a film's final budgetary success. Other contracts have to be negotiated carefully, as not to put the picture over budget and/or cause friction between producer and artist. Clearly, then, we'll have to take a close look at these five contracts:

1. Director's contract
2. Actor's contract
3. Star's contract
4. Cinematographer's contract
5. Music/Composer's contract

Director's Contract

SALARY

If you are a director who is a member of DGA (Directors Guild of America) you'll have to abide by this union's *current** rules and regulations regarding salary requirements, fringe benefits, pension, and welfare payments.

1. The DGA requires that the director be compensated for a minimum number of weeks for preproduction, principal photography, and postproduction. (The number of *minimum weeks* is based upon the film's budget.)
2. If the director works for DGA minimum salary, the DGA demands that such salary as well as a minimum number of weeks be guaranteed.
3. If the picture is delayed for a period of not more than six weeks, no additional fee is due; if the film should be canceled, the director's entire salary must be paid.
4. The following payment schedule applies:
   - 20% of salary in equal weekly installments during preproduction.
   - 60% of salary in weekly installments during principal photography.
   - 10% of salary at the time of delivery of director's cut.
   - 10% of salary upon delivery of the release print.†
5. During the course of preproduction, principal photography, and postproduction, the director is prohibited from working for a third party.
6. The producer has to deposit a specified amount for pension and welfare into a DGA account.

Fringe Benefits. The director's contract covers the following fringe benefits:

- First-class transportation if shooting on location.
- First-class hotel accommodations.

---

*Regulations change whenever the union negotiates new contract requirements.
†Release print refers to the prints exhibited in theaters.

- Office and secretary during preproduction, principal photography, and postproduction.
- A car and driver during the above-listed periods.
- A trailer during principal photography.
- Additional payments (TDY)* for time spent on location.

Billing.

1. The director's name must appear on the film's front title, immediately after the producer's credit.
2. The director's name must appear on a single title card.
3. The director's name must appear on *all* one-sheets and newspaper advertisements.

Creative Control. Once you have contracted a director, you, the producer who has nurtured the film from its conception, will have to step back and watch another person bring your project to its fruition. And that, believe you me, is not easy to do.

During preproduction the director—in concert with the producer and writer—decides upon the final script, star, cast, and other issues of vital importance. These are areas that may lead to friction and disagreements. Therefore, it is almost imperative that the director's contract decide *who* has creative control—the producer or the director. Traditionally the producer exercises supervision (notice the fine line between the terms "creative control" and "supervision") over the director, but a well-known director yields, nevertheless, a great deal of artistic control.

Once a film "goes on the floor" (commences principal photography) it is the director who runs the show; you the producer have to step aside.

A director who shows little or no budgetary sensibility might insist upon an expensive—usually unnecessary—location, or be determined to include setups that add little to the film's effectiveness. If you are burdened with an overly "creative" (read: opinionated) director, pray that you have a good production manager on your side who keeps you abreast of any incidents that threaten to push your film over budget.

Director's Cut. The director has the right to supervise the editing of the film during its first cut, called the "director's cut." At times the director has

*TDY refers to payments actors receive on location for such things as travel, meals, hotel, etc.

the contractual right to two cuts. The director's cut must be completed within a certain stipulated time limit (usually three months), and once the director's cut has been delivered the director's artistic control has ended. The producer and eventually the distributor have the right to reedit the picture.

Actor's Contract

Should you plan to produce a low-budget film (below half a million dollars), and if you have decided against casting a "star" (after all, it is almost impossible to interest a "name" to work for a fee small enough to fit your budget), then you'll do well to cast nonunion actors.

It is a fallacy that SAG (Screen Actors Guild) actors are more talented or skilled than their nonunion counterparts. Many SAG actors who have little or no acting experience or training joined the union via a commercial shot by a SAG signatory company.* Let me explain: In order to be accepted by SAG as a member, an actor has to work one day on a commercial shot by a SAG signatory production firm, or three days on a SAG signatory TV show or film.

If you have cast a "star"—that is, a recognizable name—your production company *must* become signatory to SAG, which means you are permitted to cast SAG members only. You are prohibited from employing union and nonunion actors on the same shoot. Yet, if you have decided to add a nonunion actor to your cast, a letter to SAG stating your request to have the actor granted membership will take care of the membership rules.

Once your company is SAG signatory, you'll have to adhere to these regulations:

1. A SAG actor cannot work below minimum scale on a day-to-day or week-to-week basis. In addition, the producer has to pay set amounts for pension and welfare, as well as a 10 percent agent's fee on top of the actor's salary (if the contract has been negotiated by the actor's agent).

2. The SAG actor is permitted to work only a specified number of hours daily. If the actor works over the allowed time, overtime has to be paid.

*The SAG signatory company adheres to all SAG rules and regulations.

Furthermore, the actor must be provided with meals, customarily breakfast and lunch. Child actors work fewer hours. In addition, a teacher and social worker must be present on the set and/or location whenever child actors are employed.

3. If an actor has been cast for the entire duration of principal photography, and if the production does not commence on time, then a "free period" sets in, which means the actor has to render his or her time without pay. The same holds true for reshooting of scenes and looping (rerecording of dialog).

Additionally, the actor has to render his or her services free for publicity purposes, wardrobe fittings, makeup tests, and rehearsals to principal photography.

4. As far as auditions are concerned, SAG demands the following:

- The actor must be given the opportunity to pick up his or her "sides" (pages of script) at the production office three days prior to auditioning.
- Auditions are not to be paid. The same holds true for callbacks. Two callbacks are free, the third one must be paid for.

5. Actor's compensation is to be paid weekly.

6. All actors' names not appearing on the front titles must appear on the "crawl."*

Star's Contract

While actors' contracts are pretty much standard, it is your star's contract that needs your attorney's attention.

Stars, like directors, demand, and get, the usual fringe benefits:

- First-class travel if shooting on location.
- First-class hotel accommodations.

---

*"Crawl" refers to the end titles of a film.

- Additional daily payments (TDY) if shooting on location.
- A car and driver during rehearsals and principal photography.
- A trailer on the set.

As far as responsibilities are concerned, the star must give his or her time "free" for rehearsals prior to principal photography, for wardrobe fittings, makeup tests, and publicity shots. And again, even the star cannot demand any payment for loopings and reshooting of scenes. Yet, if a film goes into overtime, the star has more clout. Stars usually demand a "stop date," after which they will no longer be available. Given the fluctuating ways of film production, most producers resist the imposition of a stop date.

If a star has some measure of clout, his or her agent works diligently to establish the star's power over producer and director by demanding amendments such as:

1. The star has script and cast approval. (The wise producer tries hard to have this clause changed to give the star the right to "consultation" rather then "approval.")

2. The star's role cannot be diminished. Since this clause demands that *all* of the star's scenes in the script will be shown in the release print,* it might be a good idea to humor your star in case the film offers strong and competitive roles for other, less well-known, actors.

On the other hand, the producer should safeguard his or her rights:

1. All rights to the results of the actor's service (the film) belong solely to the producer. That is to say, the producer has the right to use the footage in which said actor appears in *any* future motion picture (sequel or otherwise).

2. In case the producer should decide to cast another actor in the role said actor had been cast for, the producer retains the right to do so—"pay or play"—as long as the producer pays the replaced actor the agreed-upon compensation. The same applies if a producer decides to use only parts of an actor's performance. It is easy to understand why actors resent the pay-or-play clause and why agents work hard to have it omitted in their star clients' contracts.

---

*Prints shown in theaters.

3. The producer retains the right to use a double for any dangerous and/or stunt scenes the actor is involved in.

4. If the star (or any actor, for that matter) should breach the agreement, the producer has the right to suspend the actor.

5. The producer reserves the right to obtain injunctive relief against the actor.

Even though "breach of contract" seems obvious on the surface (the star does not show up for work), it is difficult to prove and therefore promises to become a tricky legal matter, since breach of contract can only be established if shooting had to be suspended solely on the grounds of the actor's absence and that due to the actor's action the production company suffered a "severe loss." Take my word for it, unless you enjoy sticking your hand into a legal hornet's nest, try to solve any breach-of-contract situation amicably by shooting around the star.

- Find an alternate scene and/or location that does not require your star's presence.
- "Double" your stars by using your star's "stand-in."* Of course, you can show the stand-in's back only, or show a frontal from a safe distance. If you use "over the shoulder" shots you'll have to dub in your star's dialogue later.
- Negotiate, negotiate, negotiate with your reluctant star.

Billing. Without any doubt your star's name should appear prominently on a separate title card on the front titles. If you have cast a well-known star, and two other recognizable names of less stature, your "star" will supersede the two other names. If, however, you have cast three actors of equal name value, you may have to do a tricky balancing act.

The crucial question of any artwork (one-sheets, mats) is "above title" billing. You may face difficulties if an equally well-known name directs your film.

I suggest that you solve this problem by showing *both names* above the film's title. For example:

---

*A person looking very much like the star, and identically dressed like the star, who stands in for lighting and rehearsal purposes.

A William Directwell Film
starring
Anita Gorgeous
in
"The Guppie Attacks New York"
with
James Strongarm and Rob Muscleman

Another sensitive issue is size, type style, and color of the star's name in artwork, where type and size of letters have to be identical to the film's title. No doubt, any secondary lead will negotiate to have his or her name preceded by the word "and" on film titles and artwork:

and
Alice Sweet as Goldilocks

If you have cast a number of equally important actors (called an "all-star cast"), the "most-favored nation" clause comes into effect. This clause specifies that in case one star receives more favorable terms than the other stars, these will receive the latter star's terms as well. But make certain that the "most-favored nation" clause does not extend to billing.

Cinematographer's Contract

The cinematographer's contract mirrors the director's contract.

Music Contracts

After your film's principal photography has been completed and as you go into editing, the question of music comes up. You have three choices:

1. An original score will be composed.
2. A synchronization license has to be obtained for music that has already been recorded.

3. You'll use "canned music," music that has been recorded, and for which a synchronization license already has been obtained.

Original Score. The composer works out the film's main musical theme, music to underscore the mood of a place, situation, or character's emotion, and music needed for scene transitional purposes.

The composer is responsible for arranging and orchestrating the score, to conduct the score or electronically synthesize it. In this respect the composer—according to AFM (American Federation of Musicians)—becomes the production company's employee.

The production company is responsible for (and has to pay for) musicians, rehearsal and recording facilities, and any incidentals such as meals, pensions, and welfare.

The company owns the score and the copyright to it. If, however, the production company operates a music publishing department, such as Warner Bros. does, the composer in addition to his/her salary receives a royalty as any published composer would.

Usually the composer and the publisher divide royalties from record and sheet music publishing sales as regulated by ASCAP (American Society of Composers, Authors and Publishers). In this respect the composer should make certain that his or her contract includes a clause stating that the music publisher (not the motion picture company) takes full responsibility for payment of the composer's share of royalties.

The royalty is based on the *wholesale* price of records, tapes, discs, and sheet music.

Contractually the composer's name must appear on your film's front titles, before the producer's credit.

You see, composed music can become a major item in your budget. In some instances, it might be a better choice to use canned music, or—if you have at least somewhat of a budget—to invest in a package deal. You have two choices:

- Hire the composer on a *package basis*. You pay a flat fee, and the composer is obligated to compose, orchestrate, and record the score.
- For a *flat fee* the composer composes the music and synthesizes it. This method, next to canned music, is the most economical way to solve your music problem.

Prerecorded Music. If you are shooting a period film that requires music popular in, say, the thirties or forties you'll have to look for prerecorded music. Prepare yourself to face some hassle and—assuredly—an extraordinarily high music budget.

First determine whether the music you have your heart set on is still in copyright.* If so, you'll have to obtain a synchronization license.

Contact the U.S. Copyright Office in Washington, D.C. (Copyright Office, Library of Congress, Washington, DC 20559) to inquire about the music's original publisher. Should the music still be protected by copyright, the producer has to negotiate a synchronization license with the music publisher. (Only the publisher can grant synchronization rights; neither ASCAP nor the U.S. Copyright Office, as some people assume, is authorized to do so.)

As you apply for a synchronization license, please remember that the license applies to the music's *theatrical* (on-screen) exploitation only, and does not extend to any other use, such as recordings.

Moreover, synchronization licenses may contain restrictions on video and cable exhibition. If you wish to use a musical piece that has been *recorded* previously, the AFM will charge a reuse fee.

A synchronization license lists the following:

- Name of musical composition.
- Name of film in which the musical composition will be used.
- Name of film in which the musical composition was used (if any).

You may run into some difficulty obtaining a synchronization license for any musical piece performed on screen (such as the famous tune from *Casablanca*); it is far easier and less costly to settle on music that has been used as background music.

There are no set price scales for prerecorded music. You may have to pay a few hundred dollars for an unknown piece, or up to hundreds of thousands for a well-known song.

In any event, the search for period music may be time-consuming, frustrating, and expensive. My advice is to forgo period music and to have appropriate music composed.

---

*If the copyright has expired and has not been renewed, you may use any music without paying a license fee.

Canned Music. The most inexpensive, least time-consuming, and often most highly effective way to "score" your film is to purchase canned music. While for some of the films I produced I commissioned music to be composed, for others I used a combination of canned music and composed synthesized music. Your sound lab can provide you with a wide selection of prerecorded canned music as well as canned ambiance sounds. You'll have to pay a small fee, which may range from a few hundred to several thousand dollars.

You won't have to worry about any licensing fees, since the sound lab owns all rights to the music, by either having purchased the music or having had it composed.

Of course, you do not own the music. You have bought the *rights* to use the music in your film, and consequently you may hear the same tune in your competitor's film. But that's a chance you'll have to take.

8.

Ways and means to
finance your film:
ten sources of money

By its very nature an "investment" refers to a venture that points to potential growth, such as promised by stocks and bonds, or provides an income as CDs do. Seen in this light, investing in a motion picture is risky business indeed. Unless a film was fortunate enough to garner sufficient "advance sales" to cover at least the movie's production cost, there is no guarantee and little promise that the investors will recoup their investment or earn a small profit. One keeps wondering why people still look upon films as sources of investment. After all, the Tax Reform Act of 1986 has all but eliminated so-called tax benefits connected to motion picture investment.

The answer to this question may be that in most of us there exists a need for adventure, that certain something that makes movie people work for little reward and makes others, fortunately, invest their money in the endeavor. It may be the inherent appeal of a gamble; it may be the lure of art, or it may be just the fun of getting a glimpse of the movie industry. Just as long as you are completely honest in divulging the high-risk nature of any motion picture investment, and depending on the world's economic situation, even the small-time independent producer will be able to interest investors in his/her project, if the:

- Producer has a track record of a number of films that recouped their original investment and earned some profit.

- Producer has a track record of bringing in films on time and on budget.
- Project features a recognizable star. The star does not have to be a blockbuster name, but ought to be recognizable among film buyers and distributors.
- Genre of the film is a popular one.

There are ten primary ways to finance one's project:

1. Partnerships:
   Joint venture
   Limited partnership
2. Corporation
3. Development Financing
4. Equity Financing
5. Foreign Financing
6. Investment Contract
7. Fractionalization
8. Grants (applicable only for nonprofit ventures)
9. Network Financing
10. Bank Financing

As you work on financing your movie, one or the other of two "financing tools" may come into the picture:

Letters of Credit (LC)
Completion Bond

Partnerships

JOINT VENTURE

In a joint venture (at times called joint partnership) set up for the purpose of producing a motion picture, any of these partners may pool their monetary, creative, and business resources:

Producer
Owner of lab (printing and developing)
Owner of sound lab
Owner of firm selling raw stock
Owner of equipment rental firm (cameras, lights, sound, and grip
   equipment)
Owner of firm providing opticals
Owner of sound stage
Screenplay writer
Director
Star
Composer
Art director
Cinematographer

In a joint venture all, or a combination of, the above-listed partners, are considered active partners. Every one of the partners has agency power—one partner can bind all members in a joint venture (joint partnership). In other words, if one partner incurs debts related to the project the partnership is involved with, all partners are liable. Partners are agents for each other:

- Each partner individually can perform any service necessary to
  conduct business (this includes borrowing money).
- Each partner is personally liable for the debts and taxes of the
  partnership; in other words, if the partnership assets are
  insufficient to pay any creditors and/or IRS claims, each partner's
  personal assets are subject to attachment.

A joint venture is a fiduciary relationship; partners cannot compete in business. All partners, as has to be stated in the partnership agreement, have certain implicit rights and duties. Unless partners have agreed to share profits and losses equally, they have to agree on a sharing ratio. (The equipment rental firm, for example, may have a smaller ratio than the lab providing developing, printing, and negative cutting.)

You see, a joint venture may be either a highly effective, a treacherous way to perform business. If you are considering setting up a joint venture, look closely at your prospective partner's reliability, commitment, and

Only if your project promises some profits will lab owners be interested in participating in a joint venture. For this reason you ought to have some basic building blocks in place before you approach any of them:

- The producer must have a track record of films that came in on time and on budget, and made some profit.
- A screenplay dealing with a popular genre, and one that offers a strong promotional hook.
- Letter of interest from a reliable distributor.
- Letter of intent from a recognizable star.
- Letter of intent from a director who has a good track record.
- It helps if the producer has lined up some presales.

LIMITED PARTNERSHIP

Most motion picture partnerships operate on the principles of a limited partnership. Setting up and operating a limited partnership requires:

- Filing of a certificate with the secretary of state.
- Filing of partnership's name.
- Certain requirements regarding calling and holding meetings.

A limited partnership is composed of a group of limited partners (the investors) and one or more general partners (the producer, or producers). The limited partners, as long as they do not actively take part in the management of the partnership (production of the motion picture), have *limited personal liability*, that is to say, limited partners risk only the capital they invested.

If the picture goes over budget, the limited partners cannot be held responsible to contribute more money. It is the general partner (or partners) who has to come up with the necessary funds. If a limited partner, however, takes part in the management of the business (that is, takes over any key position such as production manager, or participates as actor), then he or she loses the limited partnership status and becomes a general partner.

Most investors interested in joining a limited partnership do so not as much because of the promise of profits to be gained from the venture but because of tax benefits.

If a limited partner's LC (letter of credit) is used to secure a bank loan, and *if* the limited partner participates in the payment of interest rates charged on the loan, then these interest payments are deductible.

Generally, under federal tax law, expenses in a limited partnership are considered *passive* (since the limited partners do not participate in the management of the business) and such *passive* expenses cannot be used to offset *active* (non-limited partnership) income.

For instance, James Bowers has invested in Eve Roberts's movie *Beach Party in Acapulco;* he is a limited, that is to say *passive*, partner. In addition, he has set up a professional corporation with other dentists. Now, James Bowers cannot deduct the monies he spent on the interest payments (on a bank loan he took to invest in the film) from the income he derives from his professional corporation (dental practice). Yet he will be able to deduct the interest payments for this Eve Roberts film from the profit he gained from having invested as limited partner in one of her previous ventures:

Limited Partnership Expenses (*passive*)
Limited Partnership income from previous film (*passive*)
Professional Corporation (dental practice) income (*active*)

If a film provides the limited partners with capital gain, such gains will be taxed as ordinary income.

Participating in a limited partnership means that the investor (limited partner) owns a certain percentage of the venture; in other words, the investor owns a *share*. These shares are considered *securities* in much the same way as stocks are considered securities. The sale of securities is regulated by the Securities and Exchange Commission (SEC) and by the individual state's Blue Sky laws.

It is imperative that you are protected by an attorney who is highly experienced in drawing up limited partnerships. If any of the SEC laws are violated, the investors not only can demand their money back but also have the right to bring criminal charges against the general partners.*

In addition, your attorney has to deal with IRS Regulation D, which protects *nonpublic* offerings. Regulation D sets up these requirements:

- General solicitation of potential limited partners is prohibited (yet you are permitted to solicit among persons you know).

---

*Check out the Blue Sky laws (so called because these laws differ from state to state) of the state you operate your business in.

- You may not advertise for limited partners.
- You may not accept more limited partners than allowed by the SEC and the state in which your limited partnership operates, or intends to operate.
- Rule 506 and Regulation D permit the offer and sale of limited partnership shares up to $5,000,000 and restrict the venture to thirty-five investors.

At times—and this needs to be verified with your attorney and tax accountant—more investors are permitted participation. These investors, called accredited investors, must be earning a yearly income in excess of a quarter of a million dollars. These prospective investors do not qualify easily, but have to undergo extensive IRS screening.

Generally, once the limited partners have recouped their investment, they split the profit 50/50 with the general partner.

Corporation

The following is a short discussion of some of the most important legal and business aspects regarding a corporation. Generally we are looking at two kinds of corporations: The corporation set up for a large company or conglomerate, and the corporation set up for the medium or small-time producer.

Every corporation, regardless of whether it may be a multimillion-dollar outfit or a small-time firm (S-corporation), has the right and capability to issue stocks. I must warn you, it might seem very tempting to raise production funds via stock issues, but in most cases it does not work, and in some cases such practice backfires severely.

First of all, no reliable stockbrokerage house will deal with stocks issued by a small-time corporation. In other cases (and I have seen them), a group of investors eager to get hold of a company that is large enough to have its stock traded, buys enough stock to be able to take over the company.

The type of corporation we will discuss is the so-called S-corporation. This corporation protects a company's president and directors from personal liability. A corporation may be set up for one film only, or it may be the home base for any number of films.

If you are interested in having an umbrella for a number of business enterprises, you may choose, as I did, to set up your motion picture company as but one "division" under an umbrella corporation. The name of my corporation, NW&H-Industries, serves as an umbrella for my film production firm "Ciara Productions, A Division of NW&H-Industries."

Needless to say, if you consider setting up a corporation, don't buy a do-it-yourself kit, but employ a knowledgeable attorney.

A corporation is a *legal entity*, and not a group of investors as the limited partnership is. This means a corporation can hold and sell property, can sue and can be sued, just like a person. In simplified legal sense the corporation *is* a person, and this means that the corporation and not its directors are liable for debts contracted by the corporation.

The information given in this section refers to California corporations, since according to the state you wish to incorporate in, rules and regulations change.

In most states three or more persons are required to apply to the secretary of state for permission to incorporate. After payment of the incorporation filing fee and initial state franchise tax, a corporation charter is granted. Such a charter provides the following:

- Name of company
- Formal statement of formation
- Type of business
- Location of principal office
- Duration (perpetual existence, 50-year life, renewable chapter)
- Names and addresses of directors

As far as stocks are concerned, the following information must be given:

1. Classes and preference of class of stock
2. Number of PAR (stated value of stock)
3. Stock structure

The corporation code requires a statement as to the number of shares the corporation is authorized to issue, as well as the breakdown of classes, if applicable (most corporations set up for the purpose of film production do not issue a series of stock).

SUBCHAPTER-S

If you the producer should decide to set up a corporation, but feel that corporate income tax structure provides disadvantages to your company, you may consider a closed corporation. At times companies deciding to incorporate are confused about the terms "close" and "closed" corporations. "Closed," at times referred to as "closely held corporations," is used to describe a corporation having a relatively small number of shareholders. While a "close corporation" issues shares, the average "closely held" does not, and has more or less been established to protect its directors from excess liability.

A subchapter-S corporation permits a corporation to retain the limited-partnership feature of being taxed as a partnership and not as a corporation. A subchapter-S permits corporate losses to flow through to stockholders, who can use these to offset active income on their income tax return. Strange as it may sound, a number of your stockholders might join your venture because of anticipated losses that may fit their tax structure. Yet in order for subchapter-S stockholders to count corporate losses against *active* income such as salary, the stockholder must participate in the corporation's activities more than five hundred hours a year.

As you set up a subchapter-S corporation, you have to be aware of these regulations:

- The subchapter-S corporation must be a U.S. corporation.
- All stockholders must be individuals, trusts, or estates. No other corporation may purchase stocks.
- A subchapter-S corporation may not admit more than thirty-five stockholders.
- None of the stockholders may be nonresident aliens.

DIRECTORS

Ownership in a corporation is evidenced by stock certificates, but ownership of stock certificates does not give a stockholder the right to participate in the corporation's management. Yet in many small corporations the owners of the business serve as directors and managing officers.

Section 204 permits stock corporations to eliminate the liability of the directors of the corporation for monetary damages. This is important to know. The provision reads: "The liability of the directors of the corporation for monetary damages shall be eliminated in the fullest extent permissible under California law." This provision, of course, has its potential application for publicly held corporations, and does not really protect directors of closed S-corporations.

VOLUNTARY DISSOLUTION OF CORPORATION

If you had set up a corporation for one film project only, it might be dissolved. The dissolution of a stock corporation is initiated by an election to dissolve. The corporation wishing to dissolve *must* file dissolution documents with the office of the secretary of state. The mailing of those documents to any other agency, state or federal, does not meet the statutory filing requirements. The documents have to be sent by certified mail with return receipt requested (always refer to the corporation number when submitting any documents for filing).

Setting up any corporation is not inexpensive, and you definitely need the services of a tax consultant, or even better, a tax attorney. (At times one can buy an existing corporation. This, of course, saves some money, but one has to beware that one does not take over the existing corporation's liabilities, tax and otherwise, as well.)

The segments dealing with limited partnership joint venture and corporation have been written to give you some basic information and advice. Yet rules and regulations pertaining to all types of partnerships are lengthy and at times complicated, and without any doubt, you need the help of an attorney and tax consultant to set up your partnership.

If you intend to finance your movie via a partnership or corporation, you'll submit an offering, as discussed in chapter 2.

It is difficult to tell whether a partnership or a corporation provides the producer with more advantages. Here are some advantages and disadvantages:

PARTNERSHIP

Advantages	*Disadvantages*
Limited partners do not necessarily have to put up funds, but *guarantee*	The general partner (you, the producer) are liable for a film's over

Advantages	*Disadvantages*
the bank loan by issuing letters of credit (LCs).	budget and other debts.
Partnerships are more easily set up than a corporation.	Limited partners are permitted to offset losses on other *passive* investment only.
Partnerships can be set up from film to film.	Limited partners lose their limited partnership status if they become *actively engaged* in the limited partnerships's business.
Among reliable partners, all working for the same goal, a venture makes a great production team.	In a joint venture, partners are agents for each other and liable for each other's debts incurred in the management of the business.
	Limited partner shares cannot be solicited publicly.

CORPORATION

Advantages	*Disadvantages*
In a corporation the corporation, not its directors, is liable for any debts incurred.	A corporation is costly to set up.
Tax-wise, a corporation may offer some advantages to stockholders.	A corporation has to adhere to stringent rules and regulations (stockholder meetings, directors, etc.).
Shares can be sold publicly, that is to say, a broker or investment counselor can interest prospective investors in your project.	

Development Financing

Every producer needs funds in order to develop his/her motion picture project. One has to spend money on optioning the literary property. A director and one or two stars have to be added to the project, and a budget and offering have to be written. In short, the entire package has to be assembled before any investors can be approached. And let's not forget the producer's overhead, office rent, utilities, secretarial services, plus costs for fax and telephone.

If you hire a WGA (Writers Guild of America) signatory screenwriter to either adapt the literary property you have optioned or to write an original screenplay, you'll have to pay a minimum of $25,000 for the script and director, and stars may charge at least $10,000 each to grant permission to have their names attached to your project. For miscellaneous expenses, you can add another $5,000. So, conservatively speaking, if you figure between $75,000 and $100,000 you're not too far off. Agreed, a small amount if one considers the millions spent on so-called low-budget films, ranging between two and five million dollars.

But you'll have to realize that none of the above fees will be recouped should the film fail to go into production. The money you have spent on developing your project is lost. And it is for this very reason that the producer faces great difficulties raising development financing. A film in production promises recoupment and maybe some profit, yet a film in development promises nothing. Understandably, investors hesitate to provide you with the funds you'll need to get your film's development off the ground. Most producers repay development investors (plus a percentage) after the production funds have been raised. Some producers, in addition, promise to pay a percentage of the net profit. Since net profits, as we have discovered, are of a rather hazy nature, such an arrangement, in my opinion, is not quite ethical.

As far as finding development investors, you'll be pretty much on your own. Understandably, since development funds are rather small in comparison to production funds, and since the "money finders"* earn between 3 and 5 percent of the located monies, they are most likely not interested in wasting time looking for development funds.

The usual suggestion of asking development monies from friends and relatives is poor advice. Borrowing money has ruined many relationships.

---

*An individual or firm who has been hired to locate funds.

It is far better to cut your development budget to the bone and pay for it yourself (or borrow the money from a financing institution). These are a few steps you might take:

- Write the budget and offering yourself.
- Hire a nonunion (but skilled) writer to write the first draft of your screenplay. By guaranteeing that the screenplay—if the film should not go into production—will revert to the writer, you may find a writer who will work for as little as $2,000. But don't fail to reserve the right to hire another screenwriter if the studio or investors should demand it.
- If you offer them a terrific screenplay featuring challenging roles, you may be able to convince stars and director to defer their development fees.

If you are in the process of searching for development money, or if, as suggested above, you have decided to finance your film's development yourself, be completely honest with yourself. Only a small number of projects in development will ever get into production. Even if a producer was fortunate enough to garner a studio development deal, he or she has no guarantee that the film will ever go into production. A studio executive may put a project into "turnabout," that is, discontinue the film's development, because too many development projects clutter the executive's desk, a better project has captured his or her interest, or (and this happens often) the studio executive in charge of your project has been dismissed and the new person arrives with an armload of development projects of his or her own.

Equity Financing

Equity financing applies only to films budgeted over ten million. Legally, the equity partnership is a limited partnership and has to adhere to all rules and regulations pertaining to any limited partnership.

Under an equity financing contract, a limited partnership hires a producer to develop the motion picture project owned by the partnership. The partnership has been set up for the purpose of financing the development of the project. Once the producer has raised the required production funds, the partnership dissolves and the partners recoup their investment plus interest. The partners, of course, are given the opportunity to form a newly set up limited partnership investing in the film going into production.

Usually partners who had participated in the equity financing and continue to participate as limited partners will receive a slightly higher percentage than other investors if they decide to continue their participation.

These investors, to be sure, will not participate in the film's profit, but do receive their interest regardless of whether or not the film breaks even. (Yet, the recoupment of the money is not guaranteed; they do stand the chance of losing their investment.)

Foreign Financing

During the past few years, once plentiful opportunities for foreign financing have all but vanished. As in the United States, many foreign countries have clamped down, if not even outlawed, once popular tax shelters. Still, if you are determined to acquire partial foreign financing, you ought to at least give it a try.

Before you give foreign financing a second thought, you should assemble:

- Completed screenplay
- Letters of intent from an acceptable director
- Recognizable stars

Your next step is to contact an entertainment law firm that has overseas connections, to inquire about investment firms operating in the country where you plan to shoot your movie. Find out as much as you can about overseas regulations and laws pertaining to partnerships (joint venture, limited partnership, corporations).

Setting up a partnership with a foreign country may give you the opportunity to take advantage of your partner's country's tax laws, which may, unfortunately, not be any more lenient than U.S. tax laws, and by the same token you have the responsibility to adhere to your host country's laws, customs, mores, and rules. Here are some suggestions regarding coproduction with a foreign country:

- You arrange coproduction with a foreign studio and/or an established production company.
- A foreign investment firm solicits investors.
- A foreign country underwrites your production (a rare event nowadays).

Regardless of the financing scenario, all foreign countries insist on the following:

- The picture must be a major production; in other words, a picture with a budget below $5 million has no chance to acquire foreign financing.
- The U.S. producer may bring an American director and two American stars to the foreign locations. All other actors have to be hired in the country coproducing the picture.
- All key personnel (production manager, camera director, script supervisor, art director, key makeup artist, wardrobe mistress) have to be hired in the country coproducing the picture.
- All key personnel must be citizens of the coproducing country.
- The film under consideration must not be detrimental to the host country.
- The film under consideration must have "national content," that is, the film's story must be related to the host country's history, social customs, mores, etc.

A producer offering to bring in half of the required budget stands a much better chance (read: only *chance*) to have the project considered by any foreign country.

Major studios and at times mini-majors, having the advantage of extensive presales in the major foreign markets, are able to arrange mutually beneficial coproductions with foreign countries such as England, Canada, France, Italy, Germany, Japan, Spain, and major South American territories. Some smaller countries—Hungary, Malaysia, and Poland, to name a few—do welcome the lesser-known production company. These countries, with struggling, or barely existing, motion picture industries, will welcome you, the producer who brings work and money into the country. Your coproduction scenario may look something like this:

Let's say you are proposing a film budgeted for five million dollars, and have signed a director who has a track record of acceptable films, and a star who, even though not of the first order, is recognizable enough. Let's further assume that your screenplay contains the demanded "national content" and will be shot in the prospective host's country. Still, you the producer have to come up with half of the production money—in our hypothetical case, the nice round sum of two and a half million U.S. dollars.

Generally your coproducer, the host country, will not come up with cash but will supply you with services. These services are provided either free or for a nominal sum, and may include lab services, use of sound stages and editing facilities, free hotel accommodations and transportation, and—if you press hard—free raw stock.

But think twice before you pack your bags and book a flight. Granted, at times if you need the mood and scenic background of the host country, a foreign coproduction is invaluable. Nevertheless, you'll have to be aware of the drawbacks you may encounter:

Language barriers. You might not be fluent in your host country's language, and obtaining production information is complicated if done via an interpreter. Moreover, your director will face the same difficulties in trying to explain moves and expressions to foreign actors.

Different working habits. You may have to accommodate yourself to a crew that might be accustomed to exceedingly long lunch hours, including siestas. You may have to pray for patience as you ask to have a prop such as a chair or small table moved from one side of the set to the other, and are forced to wait until the grip's assistant finds *his* assistant. You have to get used to local holidays, and you may even have to close your eyes to the fact that your crew brings relatives on the set during lunch hour.

Foreign actors. Since you are permitted to bring only two stars to your host country, you'll have to cast foreign actors for all other roles.

And this will prove a major stumbling block. First, you'll have to dub* these actors; second, you'll deal with stage-trained actors who are not necessarily used to working in front of a camera.

These actors tend to overproject, move too quickly, and have difficulties

---

*Dialog has to be rerecorded in English.

hitting marks (certain areas marked on the floor where an actor has to turn or stop).

So, unless you do require the foreign country's locale and mood, you are far better off to stay home and shoot within the U.S. borders.

If you are interested in a coproduction with a foreign country (not a foreign studio or production company), you should contact the respective country's consulate general (located in most major U.S. cities), ask for the federal agency—most likely called "ministry"—in charge of motion picture coproduction, and get in touch with said agency.

Investment Contract

Some investors who are wise to the fact that only a few movies show a profit, invest in a film to earn a percentage on their investments, rather than to participate in profits.

The investment contract works well for the low-budget film, if used either in lieu of a bank loan or as intermediate financing if you finance your film via fractionalization. The investment contract investors don't—as a bank will—take possession of your literary property as collateral. If collateral is requested, it should apply to the film in production only. Do *not* agree to put personally owned stocks, bonds, or real estate up as collateral. The investment contract works best as a "stopgap measure" in concert with other investment arrangements.

Fractionalization

Fractionalization means you are financing your film via advance sales.

For the small independent producer who can list a number of fairly well-selling (not terrific) films on his/her résumé and who is known as reliable, financing a low-budget film via fractionalization is a viable way of obtaining production funds. And most important, fractionalization permits you to avoid high bank interest and to gauge your film's profit scenario more realistically.

Furthermore, this particular way of financing a project lets you keep the artistic control over your film and cuts down on distribution fees and expenses.

But fractionalization is complicated at best, and should only be attempted by a producer who is well acquainted with the ins and outs of distribution.

And another word of warning: Even though fractionalization of movie rights does bring in sizable advances, you have to take into consideration that these advances may be the only money the film will ever make. Therefore, advance sales *must* cover the entire production cost, and, it's hoped, bring in some profit.

There are several steps to consider as you solicit production funds via fractionalization.

1. Have a project that promises to sell as well internationally as domestically. Keep in mind that comedies sell well in Europe but do poorly in Japan and Southeast Asia. The Scandinavian countries, as well as Spain and Germany, object to violence.

2. Unquestionably, to launch a successful advance sale campaign you should present your prospective buyers with:

- Completed (and final) script
- Recognizable star
- Recognizable director
- Budget
- Suggested ad campaign that focuses on the films
- Hook and sellable points

The funds needed for your presale campaign can be acquired through:

- Equity investment
- Short-time bank loan

3. Your proposed film will sell more easily (and make more money) if you can prove future domestic theatrical distribution. At this point a distributor for hire will get your film into limited distribution. His or her letter of intent (not "interest") is invaluable. (If you work with an independent distribution company and not a distributor for hire, make certain to grant them the right for domestic U.S. distribution only. Do not give them the right to sell your film for home video and cable.) You'll provide the distributor with a limited number of release prints (not more than fifty) and the usual promotional material:

- Theatrical trailer
- Radio blurb
- One-sheets
- Mats

4. Presell your film to cable. Contact the executive in charge of acquisition:

HBO
1100 Avenue of the Americas
New York, NY 10036

Movie Channel
1633 Broadway
New York, NY 10019

MTV (Pop Music)
1633 Broadway
New York, NY 10019

Showtime
1633 Broadway
New York, NY 10019

Viewer's Choice
10 Universal Plaza
Universal City, CA 91608

Cinemax
1100 Avenue of the Americas
New York, NY 10036

Disney
3800 W. Alameda
Burbank, CA 91506

Encore
11766 Wilshire Boulevard, Suite 710
Los Angeles, CA 90025

You'll arrange for a *negative pick-up deal,* a certain amount of money payable to you within a year in four equal installments.

5. Presell your film for an advance to home video. Lately home video distributors have come and gone rather quickly, but to the best of my knowledge these firms have been in the business for a long time:

Handleman Company
500 Kirts Boulevard
Troy, MI 48084
(Supplies the big retailers such as Blockbuster and Wherehouse)

Ingram Entertainment
1123 Heil Quaker Boulevard
La Vergne, TN 37086

Capital Records Video Distribution
1750 N. Vine Street
Hollywood, CA 90028

Vidcom
175 West 2700 S.
Salt Lake City, UT 85115

These are just a few names; for more information, I suggest that you consult these publications:

Video Review
902 Broadway
New York, NY 10010

Video Week
475 Fifth Avenue
New York, NY 10017

Video Business Weekly
345 Park Avenue South
New York, NY 10010

Film & Video
Optical Music Inc.
8455 Beverly Boulevard, Suite 508
Los Angeles, CA 90048

You'll receive an advance, and, if the film sells well later on, royalties. The amount of the royalty depends on the previously received advance payments, but usually will range between 10 and 20 percent of each tape's wholesale price.

6. Offer your film to those foreign buyers who have bought your films previously. Most likely you'll receive LCs to be used to secure a short-term bank loan.

Some producers, hoping to garner additional advance sales, go through the expense of attending one of the foreign film markets. I discourage this. Most likely buyers who have not bought your film before will be reluctant to invest in your proposed project. It is far more advantageous to take your completed film to a U.S. distributor specializing in foreign film sales, and have him or her represent your movie. True, you'll have to pay a distribution fee and expenses, but your film does earn some additional monies.

7. Pull your project together by forming a joint venture with a lab and sound lab.

8. Produce your film, carefully watching its budget.

9. Deliver the completed movie and collect your well-deserved reward:

- Cash in the LCs
- Collect the home video advance
- Collect the first installment of your cable negative pick-up deal
- Pay off your equity investors and/or short-term bank loan.

The above scenario takes into account that you will receive the funds arranged via presales after you have delivered the film. True, major studios and mini-majors collect the advance payments before commencing the production of their projects. Nevertheless, you the small-time independent producer will garner more advance sales if you choose the latter route.

Grants

Some beginning producers hope to finance their first project though grants. In order to do so, you ought to be aware of a few basic facts:

1. Most endowers fund nonprofit operations only. You'll have the choice of either setting up a nonprofit corporation, or applying through the channel of a nonprofit conduit that administers the grants. If a grant has been approved, the conduit retains an administration fee.

2. Your project must have been tailored for a low-budget film ($500,000–$2,000,000).

3. Your film must have artistic merit, or must be based upon a literary property of philosophical or social value.

4. The story must play in the United States.

5. The film cannot be sold, exhibited, or leased for profit.

You'll have a far better chance of having your project approved if you have some financing in place. Here are a few addresses you might be interested in:

Sundance Institute for Film and Television
19 Exchange Place
Salt Lake City, UT 84111
(in order to apply you must have some financing on hand)

National Endowment for the Arts
1100 Pennsylvania Avenue
Washington, DC 20506
(your project must have artistic merit)

National Endowment for the Humanities
806 15th Street
Washington, DC 20506

Applying for a grant is time-consuming and often frustrating. A project that might be right for one agency is wrong for another. Therefore, before you even think about applying, try to find out what the endowment office wants, talk to one of the officers, and get a general feeling as to whether or not your project might meet their requirements.

In a sense, the proposal you submit to an endowment is similar to the prospectus discussed in chapter 2. Stars are unimportant if you are applying for a grant (unless you apply to the Sundance Institute), and instead of the film's hooks you'll stress your project's artistic, philosophical, or social merit. Don't forget, an endowment is greatly interested in the script per se and the expertise of the people involved.

If you have been given a grant to shoot a documentary or educational project, you may want to consider setting up a nonprofit corporation.

NONPROFIT CORPORATIONS

Nonprofit corporations for religious, charitable, special educational, and recreational purposes are organized under the Nonprofit Corporation Law, Corporation Code, Section 5000. Section 4120 (d) states: "When submitting articles for a public benefit corporation, it is required that the client include an extra copy for transmittal to the office of the Attorney General by the Office of the Secretary of State."

If a nonprofit corporation plans to obtain tax-exempt status, it may do so under the 501(c) (4) Internal Revenue Code. If, however, the corporation does not plan to be tax exempt, it has to be established as a mutual benefit corporation.

If the nonprofit corporation is supposed to be tax exempt, you'll have to take the following steps:

- Pay the minimum state franchise tax and apply for exempt status immediately after incorporation.
- Hold for delayed filing until the exemption has been granted by the state tax board.

In both cases you'll have to submit to the office of the secretary of state the articles of incorporation, consisting of an original and four copies.

Network Financing

One way of linking up with possible investors is through computer-based networks. Investors list the deals they are interested in, and the networks search for companies that meet the criteria.

Most networks charge a listing fee to both investors and companies. The success of each search, of course, cannot be guaranteed. Networks search for deals, they do not consummate them.

It is most unlikely that a producer offering his first venture will find success, but networking is a rather new and innovative way of raising funds for the producer who can look back upon several successful films.

Obtaining venture capital via network financing is not an easy task. One may count on from about six to ten months to find investors. And, of course, finding an investor is still a matter of luck. Yet, since networks run continually new applications from investors and venture capital seekers alike, your firm sees continued introduction. Once an investor has been found, and venture capital has been obtained, networks charge no fee. This is, compared to the usual finder's fee of 3 to 5 percent, a very favorable picture indeed.

The bad news is that investors participating in network programs do expect an annual return on their money of 20 percent; they are not as patient as the institutional (limited partnership) investor, and are less focused—what is hot for them one year may be uninteresting the next.

Furthermore, if these investors actually become involved in your firm (strategic partners), they have the power to take over your firm. For this reason it is imperative to find strategic partners who understand and appreciate the motion picture industry.

Networks are neither investment advisers nor brokers, and since they are unable to evaluate or verify the accuracy of the submitted application you, the producer, have to check out your prospective investors thoroughly.

This is how networks operate:

- Investors submit their interest profiles, describing their investment criteria.
- Entrepreneurs submit investment opportunities, background of their firms, a business plan, and financial projections. (Tailor your proposal to the offering discussed in chapter 2.)
- Networks submit to investors only those entrepreneurs profiled that meet their investment criteria.
- After networks have introduced investor and entrepreneur, their role terminates.

What you should know about the investors participating in networks:

- Most investors are individuals of means.
- All investors invest only in products and services promising significant growth.

- Investors *never* invest in the absence of any business plan.
- Investors insist upon a management team of proven competence and background.
- Investors need a time frame as to when they can cash in on their investments.
- All investors must certify that they are accredited investors, as defined in rule 501 in SEC regulation D, or rule 506 of regulation D.

An entrepreneur has the best chances of locating investors' monies if he or she falls into one of the following categories:

- Entrepreneurs who require venture capital between $50,000 and $1,000,000.
- Entrepreneurs whose ventures promise substantial capital gains for investors.
- Entrepreneurs with a solid and proven background in their respective fields.
- Entrepreneurs who are referred to networks by accountants, attorneys, and bankers.

What the motion picture producer needs when contacting a network:

- Solid background in motion picture production
- At least one produced financially acceptable film
- An offering (as discussed in chapter 2)
- A distribution contract and distribution plan
- A script
- A recognizable director and/or stars
- Presales sale (helpful but not necessary)

Bank Financing

Permit me to begin this section with a warning: For you, the independent producer, financing your movie via a bank loan ought to be a measure of last resort, and should be attempted only if you have been blessed with a distribution contract that provides you with an advance equaling the production cost of your film, or if you were fortunate enough to negotiate a "negative pick-up" that guarantees you an amount in excess of the production cost (cable).

Banks traditionally grant loans on the basis of "ongoing business"; that is, they grant loans to a business promising "future performances" (future loans). For this very reason, institutions such as Bank of America, Wells Fargo Bank, and Chemical Bank provide lines of ongoing credit to major studios and mini-majors. Therefore, it is easy to understand why independent producers face difficulties obtaining a bank loan. But while it is difficult to finance a film via a bank loan, it is *not* impossible if you have the following in place:

- A distribution contract (letter of intent) with a major studio or financially solvent mini-major

or

- Sizable presales of your movie to foreign distributors, domestic home video, and cable
- A well-known star
- Completion bond
- A sizable budget. It is far easier to obtain a loan for a relatively high-budget film in comparison to its lower-budgeted counterpart. Administrative costs for a film budgeted at about $2 million are identical to the ones for a film ranging in the tens of millions, or so banks claim.

A few years back, and the opportunity may arise again, banks did consider smallish production loans, the so-called secured loans. A secured loan refers to a loan secured by collateral—by the producer's film. In many cases, however, banks also demanded real estate, stocks, or bonds as additional collateral.

Motion picture loans are high-risk loans, and since banks have been burned numerous times, they approach these loans cautiously and conservatively. For this very reason the producer who intends to produce a "rock-bottom budget" picture on a budget of about $500,000 to $750,000, should not even think of approaching a bank.

It is a fact that a bank won't finance a venture unless the loan is secured substantially by low-risk real estate, blue-chip bonds, and stocks. So, instead of putting up your (and your friends' and relatives') life savings for collateral, it is far more sensible to finance your film via a joint venture instead of a bank loan.

Policies regarding motion picture financing loans vary from bank to bank, and at times from film project to film project, but most likely the bank will protect its loan by requiring the following:

Rights to the literary property (screenplay)
Security interest
Pledge-holder agreement
LCs
Completion bond

Security interest. If a film is to be shot within the United States, the bank granting the production loan files its security interest at the producer's place of business (state and county).

If the film is to be shot outside the United States, the bank will file security interest in the respective country or countries. In addition, the bank will file security interest in all documents pertaining to the film (copyright of literary property, star contracts, and so on).

Pledge-holder agreement. In case of the producer's default, labs (and other service companies) have the legal right to place liens on the film they supplied services for.

Besides taking security interest in the film, banks secure their loans through pledge-holder agreements whereby the pledge holders subordinate their liens on the film to the bank.

Furthermore, if the labs are not suppliers but participants in the venture, they—as any other participants, such as investors, director, writer, and star—are considered *unsecured* participants who, in case of the producer's default, have no rights concerning recoupment. Wise to this fact, third parties often demand recoupment and/or profit participation from any monies that have been gained via advance sales.

If third-party stipulations exist, the bank must be notified at the time of the loan application.

Letters of credit. Occasionally if a mini-major finances your movie, or if you have secured funds via private investment (partnerships), letters of credit (LCs) enter the picture. If the mini-major keeps a substantial line of credit with a bank, the bank will accept the mini-major's LC for an unsecured loan. (An unsecured loan refers to a loan that is not secured by any collateral other than the LC.)

If, however, the loan has been granted to a partnership, and participants put up LCs to secure the loan, we are speaking about a *secured* loan.

In this instance the partners' LCs have to be secured by assets, such as deposits the partners may have at the bank or the partners' stocks, bonds, and real estate.

LCs are discounted in the same way as secured loans are discounted.

Most mini-majors and private investors would much rather furnish the producer with LCs than loans. An LC serves as a *guarantee*; in case the producer should default, the bank has the LCs and the assets they represent. On the other hand, the investor issuing the LC does not have to put up any monies, as the LC serves as collateral. Should the producer, however, default on repaying the monies owed to the bank, the investor's LC will be called in.

Besides securing a bank loan, the LCs serve another purpose. As we have learned in the chapter dealing with distribution, a foreign buyer who has purchased the rights to your film will issue an LC drawn upon his or her bank, with your bank. On the LC's due date, and if you have delivered all materials to the buyer's satisfaction, you'll cash in the LC.

Completion bond. Banks don't care whether or not your film makes any money. No matter what its profitability may be, banks collect healthy interest rates; however, they are very much concerned that your film may not be completed. After all, an uncompleted film spells a loss for them, and therefore banks require completion bonds to be in place before granting or even discussing a loan.

The bonding company, like the bank, makes stringent demands. The producer has to submit:

Screenplay
Budget
Star names
List of key personnel

Interestingly enough, it is neither the popularity of the star nor the excellence of the screenplay that determines whether or not a completion bond will be granted, but the producer's track record.

A completion bond adds about 10 percent to the budget. If the film stays within the budget—and it had better if you have hopes of remaining a working producer—most bond companies agree to refund a certain percentage.

The producer has to agree to have the bonding company's representative on the set. Even if somewhat disconcerting at times, the observer's presence is a blessing in disguise. An unbiased observer notices danger areas pointing to production slowdown or over budget sooner and much more easily than the producer does.

At times, reluctantly, a bonding company takes over a production that threatens to get out of control. Then the bonding company has the right to:

- Adjust and/or rewrite the script
- Replace key personnel (including the producer)
- Replace creative personnel (including the director)
- Adjust shooting schedules
- Omit special effects and/or stunts

Unfortunately, no bank will grant funds covering the entire amount requested. In the same manner as if you were to borrow money for a real estate venture, the bank "discounts" the loan. Usually the bank discounts about 20 percent of the assessed value (that is to say, your film's budget) and it is obvious that the producer needs additional financial sources, all involving third parties:

- The producer may go into partnership with a lab and sound lab, provided their services are part of their investment.
- The producer forms a joint partnership with investors.
- The producer forms a limited partnership with investors.

Securing a bank loan is costly. You'll pay between 2 and 3 percent above the prime rate. Considering that it may take between two and three years until the bank loan plus accrued interest has been paid off, you are looking at a rather sizable amount of money. For this very reason, do not fail to include the interest rates to be paid in your budget.

In the last analysis, and don't kid yourself about it, the producer assumes the responsibility for the loan—a heavy burden indeed.

Some Tough Questions You'll Have to Answer

1. *How much money do you need?* Be very specific about the amount of money you'll need. Before approaching any possible investors, have

a realistic, if conservative, budget on hand. And most important, be
ready to discuss each item on your budget.

2. *How are you going to pay back the loans?* Be ready to provide a credible
cash-flow projection that takes the risky nature of any film venture
into consideration.

3. *Will the investors see any profit?* Do not make empty promises, but
again point to the risks involved in investing in a motion picture.
On the other hand, however, do not fail to stress your movie's sales
potentials (cable, home video, foreign).

4. *How will investors be protected?* Make it clear investors invest (and
gamble) in a high-risk venture. Don't be too ready to give any of
them collateral rights in any equity other than the film to be
produced.

Financing Terms

Angel. A private investor who is willing to provide some seed money to a
venture.

Seed money. Funds used to start out.

Asset-based loan. A loan that is tied to a firm's accounts receivable. The lender
has the right to seize the firm's assets if the borrower defaults.

Equity. Capital that entitles the investors to an interest in the firm.

Senior debt. In the event of default, the bank that granted the loan has seniority
over other investors.

Subordinated debt. A nonbank debt that stands in second position after the
bank's right to recover. These loans are also called unsecured loans.

Before you make a financing decision, here are essential points to raise with
your accountant and attorney:

- Advantages and disadvantages of the corporation—PD agreement
(pages 76–77).
- Advantages and disadvantages of the producer—PD agreement
(pages 77–78).
- What to ask about the PD agreement (page 81).
- Specifics of the pick-up deal (pages 89–93).

- Things to remember about the independent distributor's distribution contract (page 97).
- How to find out about the independent distributor's strength (pages 98–99).
- What to know about auxiliary sales (pages 100–101).
- Foreign film market distribution fees and chain of sales (pages 103–105).
- What to find out about the prospective home video distributor (page 108).

9.

A special niche:

how to market your

home video

Two types of marketing are evident in the home video market: theatrical film rental and *sell-through*. Most nontheatrical home videos (exercise, how-to, self-help, educational, and children's tapes) are sold and bought like books or records. But in no way can the nontheatrical home videotape compete with the tape output of an even mildly successful film. At the time of this writing, the nontheatrical video market commanded only a rather small fraction of the entire video output. The average number of units sold ranges between five hundred and five thousand tapes.

The immense success of Jane Fonda's famous exercise tape is not a typical example. Jane Fonda is a major movie star, and her tape was one of the first exercise tapes on the market. On the other hand, there are hundreds of tapes on the market selling well, if in conservative numbers. To name a few:

The Secret Leopard
National Geographic
Vestron Video

Arnold Palmer
Course Strategy
Vestron Video

Michael Caine
On Acting
Ingram Video

If marketed ingeniously in specialty stores, drugstores, bookstores, and (depending on its wider appeal) in major chain stores, the attention-getting packaged and professionally produced nontheatrical video still brings in a respectable profit.

Therefore, before you decide upon producing your nontheatrical tape, consider its success factors:

Marketability
Outlets
Packaging

Marketability. Because of the relatively few units sold in each outlet, your nontheatrical video *must* attract a number of different markets. To arrive at an overall marketability picture of your video, ask yourself these questions:

1. Does my nontheatrical video fall within an easily recognizable category such as exercise, cooking, or inspirational, or does it deal with a topic that, so far, has escaped extensive video representation? How about thinking of a home video exploring your own expertise in crafts, sewing, modeling, interior decorating, painting, or any other topic that can be shown visually, and—maybe even more important—has escaped extensive video representation.

2. Has your video a promotional hook? In the case of the nontheatrical video, the term "hook" does not refer as much to the participation or endorsement of a major star as it does to a "presold" audience. For instance, a tape on dog training will appeal to a fairly large group of potential buyers, while a tape on lace making will find few, if any, aficionados. If you, however, *give lectures* on an esoteric subject, such as porcelain painting, and you sell the tape during your lecture, a handsome profit can be made from moving only a few tapes.

If you've answered the above questions affirmatively, you should think about the right marketing outlets for your video:

Home video distributor
Wholesaler
Direct sales to retailer
Catalogs

Self-distribution:
TV and radio spots
Magazine coupons
· Direct mail

Home video distributor. Home video distributors have to move large numbers of units within short time periods. These units, like books and records,
must make a profit during their initial release. If a title does not sell quickly
enough, it will be backlisted, that is to say, the title will still be carried on the
packages of the distributor's sales pamphlet, but it won't be promoted any
longer. Since distributors have to sell large quantities of tapes during a short
period, understandably they are not interested in nontheatrical videos that
sell slowly but usually have a long shelf life. Yet, you may have just the kind
of tape a distributor wants to sell. As with a distributor who intends to sell
your theatrical feature film video, you'd have to sign a distribution contract.
Less complicated than the PD agreement, it still covers clauses worthy of
your, and your attorney's, consideration.

Home Video Distribution Contract

1. *Exclusive rights.* According to the agreement, the distributor handles all
areas. Have these areas spelled out, and if possible keep (after a reasonable
window*) direct sales for yourself. (Remember, the distributor loses interest
after your tape's initial surge, and your tape might languish in the company's
warehouse.)

2. *Advance.* Chances are, the advance is all the money you'll ever see.
Ask for an advance substantial enough to compel the distributor to generate
sufficient promotion for your tape. Advances, in most cases, are not paid until
the tape's *release date.* Have the distributor agree upon a specific release date.
Distributors, hoping for a "hot property" to come their way, prefer to keep
a tape release date rather vague. This is unfair; after all, the producer's funds
are tied up in the tape. Should the distributor refuse to set a release date, have
him or her pay half of the advance upon signing the agreement, and the other
half upon the tape's release.

---

*"Window" refers to the time period that has to elapse before a show can move on from one
medium to the next.

3. *Royalties.* Once the advance has been recouped, the distributor has to pay royalties to the producer. Royalties usually are based upon the nontheatrical tape's wholesale price. I suggest that instead of a percentage, your attorney arrange for a fixed dollar amount to be paid per unit.

4. *Returns.* The distributor understandably does not pay royalties on returned tapes. Expecting returns, the distributor holds back about 20 to 30 percent of the expected royalties. This sum is called a "reserve." A distributor likes to hold the reserve until all unsold tapes have been returned. It is a good idea to add a clause limiting the reserve period to six months.

5. *Delivery date.* Delivery date refers to the date the producer has to deliver the master tape and other materials to the distributor. Do not delay. Do not ask for an extension. Distributors are on tight schedules. They have to deal with graphic designers and printers (box covers, sell sheets, mats), tape duplication, and trade magazine advertising. The distributor cannot afford to miss any deadline, and neither can you if you want to stay in business.

6. *Agreements and clearances with third parties.* List all parties to whom you owe deferments, or who own points in your project. These parties may include actors, writers, labs, or private investors.

7. *Conditions precedent.* List of conditions that, if not met, render the contract null and void (have your attorney negotiate each and every clause listed).

8. *Indemnity insurance.* Most likely the distributor carries an umbrella indemnity insurance. The average how-to or self-help tape does not require such insurance.

9. *Legal documents:*

Copyright certificate (U.S. copyright registration certificate issued by the Library of Congress, Washington, D.C.).
Notarized assignment of rights (only if applicable).

10. *Governing law.* Arbitration and/or legal actions in case of disagreement.

11. *Delivery materials*:

Digital master in NTS Format
Digital video master in PAL Format.*
Music and effects track (if applicable)
Music cue sheet (if applicable and if composed music has been used)
Color slides
Black-and-white prints

12. The producer's rights to audit the distributor's books.

13. *Payment schedule*. If the producer receives an advance, you'll have to negotiate its payment:

Entire advance due at time of signing
Entire advance due at time of release
Half of the advance due at time of signing, the other half due at time of release

14. *Royalty statements*. Usually royalty statements are due biannually.

The success of any nontheatrical video may be attributed to the producer's choice of distributors; in short, a specialized tape needs a specialized distributor:

Educational Tapes

Teaching Films, Inc.
21601 Devonshire Street
Evanston, IL 60202

BFA Educational Media
468 Park Avenue South
New York, NY 10016

Library Video Company
P.O. Box 4051
Philadelphia, PA 19106

*NTS and PAL formats refer to tape formats. If your tape is to be distributed domestically, you do not need a PAL.

How-to Tapes	Do It Yourself 712 Euclid Avenue Charlotte, NC 28203
Children's Tapes	Kid Time Video 2340 Saetelle Boulevard Los Angeles, CA 90064
	The Video Schoolhouse 167 Central Avenue Pacific Grove, CA 93950
	Crown Video 225 Park Avenue New York, NY 10003
	Children's Video Library 1010 Washington Boulevard Stamford, CT 06901
Cooking	The Kitchen 512 W. 19th Street New York, NY 10011
Inspirational	Faith for Today 1100 Rancho Conejo Boulevard Newbury Park, CA 91320
	Spring Arbor Distributors 10885 Textile Road Spring Arbor, MI 48111

Wholesalers. To sell your tape via a wholesaler requires that you not only produce the tape, have it duplicated, and packaged, but also supply advertising materials. You have to supply advertising materials such as posters, cutouts, sell sheets, and, if you wish to have your tape advertised in any of the video trades, mats.

My video film *Night of Terror* (Ciara Productions, Inc., and Westlake Studios) was marketed successfully through wholesalers. We supplied the wholesaler with the boxed product and usual advertising material (sell sheets, posters and mats, but no cutouts), and once the contract was signed participated in advertising the video with one-page ads in some of the leading video trades.

Video Magazine
460 W. 34th Street
New York, NY 10001

Video Software Dealer
5519 Centinela Avenue
Los Angeles, CA 90066

Video Review
902 Broadway
New York, NY 10020

Both production firms and the wholesaler participated in the advertising cost. After about three months the film had run its course, and the returns came in. Rather than have the video backlisted, the film, as had been arranged contractually, reverted back to us. So did the returned copies. For another six months we sold the film directly through discount distributors.*

But getting back to the nontheatrical video: Unless you have a "line of titles" (that is to say, a number of subject-related nontheatrical tapes), it is difficult to convince any wholesaler to carry your product. Generally, wholesalers prefer to work with big established distributors guaranteeing a constant stream of products. In order to interest distributors in your tape, you'll have to give them a deal they cannot refuse. A 50/50 cut between producer and wholesaler off the tape's wholesale price is considered a fair deal, and the 40/60 cut is not unheard of. On top of this, a number of wholesalers want you to pay for shipping charges to retailers. Stand firm on this issue; pay shipping charges to the wholesaler only.

How acquisition works. Start out by calling distributors and wholesalers to find out who is in charge of acquisition. *Never* send out your tape and letter of inquiry cold; contact the person in charge of acquisition by phone. I prefer to establish a phone contact because I think a phone call is more personal,

*See "Fractionalization," page 141.

and it tells me immediately whether or not a company is interested in my film or tape. (When you call, don't ever permit the receptionist to pawn you off to a second-string executive.) Most likely you will be invited to mail in your tape plus some information about your company. Don't ever approach any distributor and/or wholesaler with a demo tape that shows what the final tape will be like, but supply a finished and polished product. If you intend to sell your tape via a wholesaler you must be able to show box cover and advertising materials. But box cover and advertising materials are *not* necessary if you hope to sell your tape through a home video distributor. Once your tape has aroused the acquisition department's interest, you'll be invited to a meeting. This meeting will be a short one, and you'll have to push your tape's hook. Refer to the tape's most salient points only; do not permit yourself to ramble on about secondary issues. Remember, the acquisition department is not interested in your tape's merits, it is interested in your tape's sellability.

If acquisition has been properly impressed by your tape and your presentation, the marketing department comes onto the scene. Once you are dealing with marketing, prepare yourself to deal with pointed questions:

- Who will buy your tape?
- Has the tape been geared toward a distinct group of buyers?
- What specific feature, topic, or tool will attract them?
- Will enough tapes be sold to justify marketing cost and effort?
- How much will it cost to put the tape on the market?
- What is the likely profit margin?

Retailers. First of all, don't even *think* about selling your nontheatrical tape to your kindly neighborhood video store. True, this store—like any other video rental store in the country—does do a booming business. But it *never* buys from an individual producer; it orders its supplies from wholesalers. And don't forget, your neighborhood video store is in the rental business, making a living by renting out tapes of feature films. A video retailer cannot afford to clutter precious shelf space with nontheatrical tapes renting only a few times. And besides, how many video stores will you be able to contact? Granted, there are mailing lists galore. You can purchase a mailing list, each giving about 200,000 names and addresses of video rental stores. But mailing out your nontheatrical video is nothing but an enormous waste of money. Generally, one expects about 1 to 2 percent return answers from a mailing list. I would not count on even that small number; the average corner video retailer does not buy from individual producers.

If your tape has strong general appeal, you may consider contacting large chain stores such as Montgomery Ward, Sears, K mart, Wal-Mart, and so on. Concentrate on their merchandise that ties in with your tape. Here are a few examples:

- Dressmaking in a jiffy—fabric chain stores
- Gourmet cooking, fast cooking, inexpensive cooking, inexpensive entertaining—housewares and/or appliance department
- Interior decorating on a budget—furniture chain stores

Give it some thought; there are hundreds of possibilities for the savvy producer. Contact the chain's corporate headquarters and ask for the executive in charge of the department you have targeted.

Naturally, as with selling to wholesalers you'll have to supply the chain with the duplicated tape, including box, as well as some posters.

The drawback is, if the chain store does not employ an internal distribution system, you'll have to ship your tapes to each and every individual store. And this, believe me, is lots of hard work. You'll have to concern yourself with getting the tape duplicated, packaged, and shipped,* as well as billing and collecting.

If you have produced a nontheatrical tape wide enough in general appeal to interest the countless minimalls dotting the country, you may want to get in touch with a wholesaler specializing in this field:

Handleman Company
500 Kirts Boulevard
Troy, MI 48084

On the other hand, if you have a highly specialized tape that may be combined with a book of the same topic, your best bets are bookstores. Here I would suggest that you do not try to contact the major chains (Crown, WaldenBooks, Bookstar, B. Dalton) directly, but work through a distributor highly experienced in this genre:

---

*You may, of course, select to have packaging and shipping done by a fulfillment house. We will discuss this method under TV sales.

Ingram Video
1123 Heil Quaker Blvd.
La Vergne, TN 37086

But be forewarned, bookstores expect 60 percent off the retail price, and they do have a 100 percent return policy. But, on the other hand, if your tape or book-tape combination finds enough friends, it will enjoy a long shelf life.

I successfully sold my nontheatrical tape *The Beginning Director's Guide to Filmmaking,* based on the book of the same title, through several chains specializing in home video equipment.

Catalogs. During the past years catalogs selling a variety of merchandise have become very popular. The most recent additions are catalogs selling home videos. To get acquainted with numerous catalogs you may check *Publisher's Source Book,* which you'll find in your local library, or write to:

Videotape Catalog
SMW Video Inc.
803 Russell Boulevard #2
Davis, CA 95616

I'd suggest that you call a catalog's acquisition department to find out whether the company is interested in your video's topic. If so, follow up with a letter stating:

- Target audience.
- Reasons why the target audience should be interested in your tape.
- Your tape's hook.
- In what way your tape is different (and better) from other tapes dealing with the same genre, or the reasons why a tape offering a new topic should find viewers' favorable response.

Don't forget to list a number of possible follow-up tapes; let the catalog company know that if your tape sells well you are ready with a stream of products. Catalogs, like wholesalers, are more interested in prolific producers.

*Walker and Company, 435 Hudson Street, New York, NY 10014

Catalogs are mailed out every two months, and your tape will be carried in one or two issues. You should expect to sell between 500 and 1,000 units. The producer *does not* participate in the catalog's printing and mailing cost, but has to supply the catalog with two or three color slides, mats, and two or three black-and-white pictures.

The catalog expects a 60 percent discount of the tape's retail price, and has a 100 percent return policy.

My company, Ciara Productions, Inc., in partnership with Udell Studios and a German company, Schau Mal TV, produced a made-for-video comedy in German, *Rote Tasche (The Red Satchel)*. The tape was marketed successfully through catalog sales. These catalogs were sent to German bookstores and specialty stores, as well as to individual customers who had purchased tapes previously.

Sponsors. A highly lucrative way of selling your nontheatrical video is sponsor tie-in. Granted, the process of convincing a sponsor about your tape's viability is difficult and frustrating. After all, your tape is supposed to make the customer choose the sponsor's product over another manufacturer's product or service. Therefore, you have to be specific about what the tape offers.

1. Exposure of the sponsor's merchandise and/or services.
2. Exposure of the sponsor's logo.
3. The promise that the tape will interest customers to buy more of the sponsor's services or merchandise.
4. The viewer's favorable association between tape and sponsor's service or merchandise.
5. The promise that the viewer has reason to view the tape more than once; this way the sponsor's name is kept in the viewer's mind.

As you are dealing with a prospective sponsor, do not offer a produced tape, but manufacture one to order. (It helps if you can point to a line of your tapes that has been marketed through catalog sales, distributors, wholesalers, or chain stores.) In any event, you must demonstrate your experience and professionalism in the field of the nontheatrical tape. Once you approach your prospective sponsor, you'll have to present a fully detailed outline.

For instance, let's assume you are pitching a tape idea on home protection. You'll not only stress the tape's topic but the following as well:

1. As the sponsor advertises and keeps booths at various home shows throughout the country, the tape (showing the sponsor's name and logo) will

be displayed prominently. The tape can be shown on a big-screen TV throughout the day.

2. The tape will show the sponsor:

- providing security guards for special events.
- providing special security for apartments, condos, banks, malls, businesses.
- providing twenty-four-hour security for private homes, and special security if owner is on vacation
- providing security (special telephone numbers and/or a calling device) for shut-ins and the elderly

3. In this way a client who has contracted one service will be exposed to the company's additional services.

4. Stress that a tape is far more successful and not more expensive than a four-color brochure, since it talks to the viewers directly. It acquaints them with the skilled and helpful people employed by your company.

This is the most important point of your presentation. The tape should not be viewed once and thrown away (as a brochure might) but should be *consulted* by the viewers. Therefore, the tape must contain information that warrants repeated viewing, such as:

- how to make your home burglar-proof
- how to make your home burglar-proof when you go on a short or extended vacation
- what to do and not to do when mugged
- how to avoid being mugged
- safety devices for your home, car, and on your person

You may encounter a sponsor that likes your idea but feels there are not enough video players around to make the tape-premium campaign successful. You counter with the answer that individuals and/or firms considering the firm's service or merchandise most likely own a VCR.

Once you set your mind to it, you'll find a number of sponsors to contact. Here are a few examples:

Sponsor	*Suggested Tape*
Banks (to new customers)	Saving and budgeting money

Sponsor	*Suggested Tape*
Health food chain	Nutrition and good health
Health spa chains	Exercise tape with a new twist

Before you contact a sponsor, find out whether your prospective client works with an in-house advertising department, or deals with an advertising agency exclusively. If the latter is the case, you ought to contact the agency before even speaking to the sponsor about your project.

Fractionalization. If you have signed with a distributor or agreed to have a wholesaler sell your tapes, don't forget to keep a window open, entitling you to direct and catalog sales.

Once your tape has run its course in a catalog, its life is not over by any means. Now the discount wholesalers come into the picture:

Budget Video
1540 N. Highland Avenue
Los Angeles, CA 90028

Discount Video Tapes
500 S. Buena Vista Street
Burbank, CA 91521

Movie Tape Exchange
9380 Route 130 North
Pennsauken, NJ 08109

Video Shuttle Nework
445 Eighth Avenue NW
St. Paul, MN 55112

Video Closeouts of America Inc.
261 Central Avenue, Suite 42
Jersey City, NJ 07307

Your profit margin, of course, is small. The discount firm sells your tape for about half of its former wholesale price.

Selling your tape via radio and TV spots. Both TV and radio spots can be immensely successful in bringing a product (your tape) to the public's eye, *if* your budget is big enough to carry the advertising expense, and *if* the number of units selling justify the expense.

TV spot. Producing a thirty-second commercial, conservatively speaking, costs between $10,000 and $20,000 even if you have no known star attached.

Naturally you want to bypass the prime-time spots and have your commercial shown at "preexemptible time," that is, during late-night hours. Rates vary. Naturally a commercial shown on a Scotts Bluff, Nebraska, TV station is far less expensive than one airing in Los Angeles or New York.

Radio spots. Advertising on radio is far less expensive than advertising on TV. Radio reaches a smaller but more specified audience, and before placing any spots you must know the demographics of the particular station—find out about the age and socioeconomic groups most likely to tune in. The best time slots are during rush hours, when drivers stuck in gridlock turn to their radios for solace.

TV and radio spots sell best if you provide the public with an 800 number to call. Flash the 800 number during the last ten seconds of your commercial. Make the number easy to remember; people do not have time (or in the case of radio advertisements, the opportunity) to get pencil and paper. Something like 1–800-GET TAPE might do the trick. For the very same reason *do not* list an address for customers to write to.

The 800 number, of course, demands that operators are on duty when your TV spot airs. This in turn demands that you work with a fulfillment house that processes the called-in orders and ships them out. Shipping charges change from company to company, but generally you'll have to count on:

$1.25 for processing order
 1.25 for invoice
  .25 for box and packing materials

The additional UPS charges have to be paid by the customer.

Mailings. Direct mailing used to be a highly effective sales method. But lately, as everyone faces an avalanche of advertisements, its appeal fades quickly. Most of the letters and brochures end up *unread* in the wastepaper basket. None of us has the time and inclination to read about goods and services we don't need and do not want to know about. The key to an effective direct mailing is that you obtain a list addressing exactly the clientele you wish to contact.

You may wish to contact the following publications:

Direct Mail List Rates and Data
Standard Rate and Data Service, Inc.
3004 Glenview Road
Wilmette, IL 60611

The Direct Marketing Association, Inc.
6 East 43rd Street
New York, NY 10017

The Direct Market Place:
The Directors of the Direct Marketing Industry
c/o Hilary House Publishers, Inc.
980 North Federal Highway, Suite 206
Boca Raton, FL 33932

Direct Marketing News
c/o DMN Corp.
19 W. 21 Street
New York, NY 10010

Direct mailing is expensive. First, you'll have to consider the cost of your brochure, which may run between $2,000 and $10,000. These costs include:

Copywriter (you may do this yourself)
Typesetting
Artwork (graphic art, color separation)
Printing

True, you may elect to design a single-sheet ad and have it photocopied. The cost will be minimal, but you'll still have to concern yourself with postage. And postage is sky high, if you consider that the average mailing list contains between 50,000 and 200,000 names. Further, you ought to consider that the average response to direct mailing falls below 1 percent.

Yet, on the positive side, direct mail permits you to build a basic group of clients interested in repeat purchases.

Magazine ads. Instead of direct mailing you might look at magazine ads that include an order coupon as a way to build your clientele. You will, naturally, advertise only in magazines catering to the specific clientele you wish to reach. Magazine advertising is not inexpensive. Fees are based upon the size of your ad, the number of times the ad appears, and upon the magazine's circulation. Here's a word of warning: Running your ad only once does not pay. You may as well save your money. In a weekly magazine, an ad should run at least for four weeks; in a monthly magazine, for three months. Rates vary greatly between national and local publications. But, and this is the good news, your ad—depending on the topic—might be far more successful in the less expensive local publication.

Packaging. The key to any successful tape—regardless of whether it's a feature film or nontheatrical tape—lies in the packaging. Sales depend to a great degree upon the eye-catching box.

Remember, the nontheatrical video does not have a well-known star, thrilling story, or popular genre in your corner. All it has to offer is topic. Therefore, the topic ought to be stressed. Here are a few points to remember:

- Know your audience.
- Catch the prospective buyer's attention.
- Give the buyer faith in your tape.
- Stress the tape's hook.
- Be precise in listing what the tape promises to deliver.

And most important: *Deliver what the tape promises.*

Title. Permit me to refer to my nontheatrical tape *The Beginning Filmmaker's Guide to Directing.* Since the tape is based on parts of the book with the above title, the book's title was used. But since the tape was sold at chains specializing in camcorders and home video equipment, the box was geared neither to the cinema student nor to the aspiring motion picture director, but to the camcorder buff who wants to improve his/her home videos. Therefore, the selling blurb "gives your home video the professional touch" refines the title.

And on the box's back cover we listed all the tricks of the trade discussed and taught on the tape.

In addition, you may want to list on the back cover:

list of credits
copyright
manufacturer's address
bar code
reviews and endorsement

It is not easy to get your nontheatrical video off the ground. It takes determination, know-how, and luck. But once you have established yourself with a selling video, you'll have it made. Producing an excellent nontheatrical video is far less expensive and time-consuming than a feature film, and you have to fight less competition.

Still, I'd like to advise you to test the market before you jump in. Do not spend any time or money producing your tape before you have checked its viability:

- Talk to possible sponsors.
- Order catalogs to get an idea about what is on the market.
- Look at top-selling tapes and evaluate their selling points.
- Browse video retail stores to see what is on the shelves.
- Browse major chain stores.
- Contact wholesalers and distributors.

If your interesting and professionally produced and packaged nontheatrical home video did not find any takers, you might consider visiting Cinetex, an annual convention of the home video industry. The convention is held at Las Vegas, Nevada. For information as to time and place, contact:

The Interface Group, Inc.
(world's largest producer of conferences and expositions)
300 First Avenue
Needham, MA 02194

Last Word
I hope this book will help you get your motion picture or home video project off the ground. And don't forget, to find financing for your movie and to produce and distribute it successfully is not an easy undertaking. It takes time, know-how, and most of all persistence and determination.

Good luck to all of you.

*A*ppendix

Film Festivals
Associations and Labor Organizations
Sample Release Form (for Screenplay)
Sample Theatrical Distribution Plan (Domestic)
Sample Standard AFTRA Performer's Employment Contract
Sample Grant Application (The Independent Film and Videomaker Program, The American Film Institute)

Film Festivals

These festivals give the filmmaker the opportunity to exhibit his or her film; however, they do not market films.

Filmfest D.C.
April 21–May 2
Washington International Film Festival
Box 21396
Washington, DC 20009

AFI International Film Festival
June 10–24
AFI Exhibitions
2021 North Western Avenue
Los Angeles, CA 90027

Toronto International Film Festival
September 8–18
Toronto International Film Festival
70 Carlton Street
Toronto, Ontario M5B

Boston Film Festival
(affiliated with Boston University)
Boston Film Festival
400 Plaza Drive
Secaucus, NJ 07094

New York Film Festival
Society of Lincoln Center
70 Lincoln Center Plaza
New York, NY 10023

Denver International Film Festival
Denver International Film Society
999 18th Street, Suite 1820
Denver, CO 80202

Associations and Labor Organizations

Academy of Motion Picture Arts & Sciences
8949 Wilshire Boulevard
Beverly Hills, CA 90211 ....(310) 247-3000

Academy of Television Arts & Sciences
3500 W. Olive Avenue, #700
Burbank, CA 91505 ....(818) 953-7575

Actors' Equity Association
6430 Sunset Boulevard, #1002
Hollywood, CA 90028 ....(213) 462-2334

Advertising Club of Los Angeles
3600 Wilshire Boulevard, #432
Los Angeles, CA 90010 ....(213) 382-1228

AFI Film Festival
2021 N. Western Avenue
Los Angeles, CA 90027 ....(213) 856-7707

AFTRA
6922 Hollywood Boulevard
Hollywood, CA 90028 ....(213) 461-8111

Alliance of Motion Picture & Television Producers, Inc.
14144 Ventura Boulevard, 3rd Floor
Sherman Oaks, CA 91423 ....(818) 995-3600

American Association of Advertising Agencies
8383 Wilshire Boulevard, #342
Beverly Hills, CA 90211 ....(213) 658-5750

American Cinema Editors, Inc.
4416 1/2 Finley Avenue
Los Angeles, CA 90027 ....(213) 660-4425

American Film Institute (AFI)
2021 N. Western Avenue
Los Angeles, CA 90027 ....(213) 856-7600

American Film Marketing Association
10000 Washington Boulevard, #5266
Culver City, CA 90232 ....(213) 275-3400

American Guild of Musical Artists
15060 Ventura Boulevard, #490
Sherman Oaks, CA 91409 ....(818) 907-8986

American Guild of Variety Artists (AGVA)
4741 Laurel Canyon Boulevard, #208
North Hollywood, CA 91607 ....(818) 508-9984

American Humane Association
14144 Ventura Boulevard, #260
Sherman Oaks, CA 91423 ....(818) 501-0123

American National Academy of Performing Arts
10944 Ventura Boulevard
North Hollywood, CA 91604 ....(818) 763-4431

American Society of Cinematographers
1782 N. Orange Drive
Hollywood, CA 90028
          and
P.O. Box 2230
Hollywood, CA 90078 ....(213) 876-5080

ANTA WEST
427 N. Canon Drive
Beverly Hills, CA 90210 ....(213) 465-5315

ASCAP
6430 Sunset Boulevard, 2d Floor
Hollywood, CA 90028 ....(213) 466-7681

Association of Film Craftsmen NABET Local 531, AFL-CIO
1800 N. Argyle Avenue, #501
Hollywood, CA 90028 ....(213) 462-7484

Association of Talent Agents
9255 Sunset Boulevard, #318
Los Angeles, CA 90069 ....(213) 274-0628

BMI
8730 Sunset Boulevard, 3d Floor West
Los Angeles, CA 90069 ....(213) 659-9109

Broadcast TV Recording Engineers Local 45, IBEW
6255 Sunset Boulevard, #721
Los Angeles, CA 90028 ....(213) 851-5515

California Film Commission
6922 Hollywood Boulevard, #600
Hollywood, CA 90028 ....(213) 736-2465

Choreographers Guild
256 S. Robertson Boulevard, #1775
Beverly Hills, CA 90211 ....(213) 275-2533

Cinematographers Union
7715 Sunset Blvd., #300
Hollywood, CA 90046 ....(213) 876-0160

505 Eighth Ave., 16th Floor
New York, NY 10018 ....(212) 244-2121

Conference of Personal Managers
4527 Park Allegra
Calabasas Park, CA 91302 ....(818) 888-8264

Costume Designers Guild
Local 892, IATSE
14724 Ventura Boulevard, Penthouse
Sherman Oaks, CA 91403 ....(818) 905-1557

Directors Guild of America
7950 Sunset Boulevard
Los Angeles, CA 90046 ....(310) 289-2000

Dramatists Guild
2265 Westwood Boulevard, #462
Los Angeles, CA 90064 ....(213) 470-3683

Film Advisory Board
7080 Hollywood Boulevard
Hollywood, CA 90028 ....(213) 874-3644

Film & Television Archive—UCLA
Los Angeles, CA 90024 ....(213) 206-8013

Film/Video Technicians
Local 683, IATSE, AFL-CIO
6721 Melrose Avenue
Los Angeles, CA 90038 ....(213) 935-1123

Friars Club of California, Inc.
9900 Santa Monica Boulevard
Beverly Hills, CA 90212 ....(213) 879-3375

Greater Los Angeles Press Club
600 N. Vermont Avenue
Los Angeles, CA 90004 ....(213) 665-1141

Hollywood Chamber of Commerce
6255 Sunset Boulevard, #911
Hollywood, CA 90028 ....(213) 469-8311

Hollywood Foreign Press Association
292 S. La Cienega Boulevard, #316
Beverly Hills, CA 90211 ....(213) 657-1731

IATSE & MPMO
14724 Ventura Boulevard, PH Suite
Sherman Oaks, CA 91403 ....(818) 905-8999

International Alliance of Theatrical Stage Employees
Local 33, IATSE
1720 W. Magnolia Boulevard
Burbank, CA 91506 ....(818) 842-9233
1515 Broadway #601
New York, NY 10036 ....(212) 730-1770

International Documentary Association
8489 West 3rd Street, #80
Los Angeles, CA 90048 ....(213) 655-7089

International Photographers
Local 659, IATSE, MPMO
7715 Sunset Boulevard, #300
Los Angeles, CA 90046 ....(213) 876-0160

International Press Association
Box 8560
Universal City, CA 91608 ....(213) 876-7773

International Sound Technicians
Local 695, IATSE, MPMO
11331 Ventura Boulevard, #201
Studio City, CA 91604 ....(213) 877-1052

Los Angeles Chamber of Commerce
404 S. Bixel Street
Los Angeles, CA 90017 ....(213) 629-0711

Make-Up Artists & Hair Stylists
Local 706, IATSE, MPMO
11519 Chandler Boulevard
No. Hollywood, CA 91601 ....(818) 984-1700

Motion Picture Association of America, Inc.
14144 Ventura Boulevard, 2d Floor
Sherman Oaks, CA 91423 ....(818) 995-3600

Motion Picture Costumers
Local 705, IATSE, MPMO
1427 N. La Brea Avenue
Hollywood, CA 90028 ....(213) 851-0220

Motion Picture & Video Tape Editors Guild
Local 776, IATSE
7715 Sunset Boulevard, #220
Los Angeles, CA 90046 ....(213) 876-4770

Motion Picture Health & Welfare Fund
11365 Ventura Boulevard
Studio City, CA 91604 ....(213) 877-0991

Motion Picture Illustrators & Matte Artists
Local 790, IATSE
14724 Ventura Boulevard, PH-B
Sherman Oaks, CA 91403 ....(818) 784-6555

Motion Picture Screen Cartoonists
Local 839, IATSE
4729 Lankershim Boulevard
No. Hollywood, CA 91602 ....(818) 766-7151

Motion Picture Studio Grips
Local 80, IATSE, AFL-CIO
6926 Melrose Avenue
Los Angeles, CA 90038 ....(213) 931-1419

Motion Picture & Television Fund
23388 Mulholland Drive
Woodland Hills, CA 91364 ....(818) 347-1591

Musicians Union
Local 47
817 N. Vine Street
Hollywood, CA 90038 ....(213) 462-2161
          and
1501 Broadway, #600
New York, NY 10036 ....(800) 762-3444

National Academy of Recording Arts & Sciences
303 N. Glenoaks Boulevard, #140 Mezzanine
Burbank, CA 91502 ....(818) 843-8233

Permanent Charities Committee of the Entertainment Industries
463 N. La Cienega Boulevard
Los Angeles, CA 90048 ....(213) 652-4680

Producers Guild of America, Inc.
400 S. Beverly Drive
Beverly Hills, CA 90212 ....(213) 557-0807

Publicists Guild
Local 818, IATSE, MPMO, AFL-CIO
14724 Ventura Boulevard, PH #5
Sherman Oaks, CA 91403 ....(818) 905-1541

Scenic & Title Artists
Local 816, IATSE
6180 Laurel Canyon Boulevard, #275
North Hollywood, CA 91606 ....(818) 769-0816

Screen Actors Guild
7065 Hollywood Boulevard
Hollywood, CA 90028 ....(213) 465-4600

Screen Cartoonists Guild
Teamsters Local 986
1616 West 9th Street, #300
Los Angeles, CA 90015 ....(213) 380-9860

Screen Extras Guild, Inc.
3629 Cahuenga Boulevard West
Los Angeles, CA 90068 ....(213) 851-4301

Script Supervisors
Local 871, IATSE
7061-B Hayvenhurst
Van Nuys, CA 91406 ....(818) 782-7063

Set Designers & Model Makers
Local 847, IATSE
14724 Ventura Boulevard, PH-B
Sherman Oaks, CA 91403 ....(818) 784-6555

Society of Motion Picture & TV Art Directors
Local 876, IATSE
14724 Ventura Boulevard, PH #4
Sherman Oaks, CA 91403 ....(818) 905-0599

Society of Professional Stuntwomen
5501 Van Noord Avenue
Van Nuys, CA 91401 ....(213) 462-2301

Songwriters Guild of America
6430 Sunset Boulevard, #317
Hollywood, CA 90028 ....(213) 462-1108

Southern California Broadcasters Association
1800 N. Highland Avenue, #609
Hollywood, CA 90028 ....(213) 466-4481

Story Analysts Guild
Local 854, IATSE
14724 Ventura Boulevard, PH-B
Sherman Oaks, CA 91403 ....(818) 784-6555

Stuntmen's Association
4810 Whitsett Avenue
North Hollywood, CA 91607 ....(818) 766-4334

Stunts Unlimited
3518 Cahuenga Boulevard West
Los Angeles, CA 90068 ....(213) 874-0050

Television Bureau of Advertising, Inc.
6380 Wilshire Boulevard, #1711
Los Angeles, CA 90048 ....(213) 653-8890

Theater Authority, West
6464 Sunset Boulevard, #640
Hollywood, CA 90028 ....(213) 462-5761

United Stuntwomen's Association
3518 Cahuenga Boulevard West, #206-A
Los Angeles, CA 90068 ....(213) 874-3584

U.S.O.
1641 Ivar Avenue
Hollywood, CA 90028 ....(213) 462-6904

Variety Entertainers Guild of America (VEGA)
1741 N. Ivar Street, #201
Hollywood, CA 90028 ....(213) 464-9134

Western States Advertising Agencies Association
2410 Beverly Boulevard, #1
Los Angeles, CA 90057 ....(213) 387-7432

Women In Films
6464 Sunset Boulevard, #660
Hollywood, CA 90028 ....(213) 463-6040

Writers Guild of America, West, Inc.
8955 Beverly Boulevard
Los Angeles, CA 90048 ....(310) 550-1000
      and
555 W. 57th St.
New York, NY 10019 ....(212) 582-1909

Sample Release Form

To be attached to any screenplay, prospectus, and/or offering submitted.

_____, 19_____
Title and/or Theme of
Material Submitted
Hereunder:

_____

_____

Gentlemen:

I am today submitting to you certain program material, the title and/or theme of which is indicated above (which material is hereinafter referred to as the "program material"), upon the following express understanding and conditions:

1. I acknowledge that I have requested permission to disclose to you and carry on certain discussions and negotiations with you in connection with such program material.

2. I agree that I am voluntarily disclosing such program material to you at my request. I understand that you shall have no obligation to me in any respect whatsoever with regard to such material until each of us has executed a written agreement, which, by its terms and provisions, will be the only contract between us.

3. I agree that any discussions we may have with respect to such program material shall not constitute any agreement expressed or implied as to the purchase or use of any of such program material, which I am hereby disclosing to you either orally or in writing.

4. In the event that you have an independent legal right to use such material, which is not derived from me, either because such material submitted hereunder is not new or novel, or was not originated by me, or has not been reduced to concrete form, or because other persons including your employees have submitted similar or identical material, which you have the right to use, then I agree that you shall not be liable to me for any use of such material and you shall not be obligated in any respect whatsoever to compensate me for such use by you.

Yours very truly,

_____

Sample Theatrical Distribution Plan (Domestic)

Low-Budget Film
Stars
Information regarding star or star's popularity.
Rating
Expected rating.
Advertising Campaign
The title is of utmost importance. The title ought to zero in on the film's hook, and it must be immediately recognizable. If the title is memorable, so much the better.
Trailer
The theatrical trailer must demonstrate the film's story and style, and ask questions that can only be answered by seeing the film.
TV Spots
TV spots are the most important campaign tool. Sixty, thirty, and fifteen-second spots should be cut, as well as a ten-second teaser. The spots ought to feature the star (stars) and the film's most visually arresting moments. A strong VO catch line pulls all elements together. TV spots are expensive, and for this reason should be purchased for frequency, rather than length of running time.
Radio
Fortunately, stations that pull in the highest number of listeners are not necessarily the most expensive in their markets. Stations usually are willing to augment a paid schedule with a sizable promotional campaign. Radio spots should focus on the film's most effective audio moments. Radio promotion requires a month's advance planning.
Poster
The poster (one-sheet, sell sheets) should be simple, slick, and immediately recognizable.
Newspaper Ads
Full-page ads are a waste of money for the average small, low-budget film. But by placing a number of ads within a thoroughly worked out schedule, the film should catch video retailers' interest.

Magazines

Magazines should play an important part in the promotion of any film because of the long lead time; however, a film released territory by territory benefits little from magazine ads. Yet, any magazine exposure generated through paid ads and (free) publicity articles will increase the film's home video release possibilities.

Press Kit

The press kit should be as slick as possible, as it is the press kit that will determine to which extent radio and TV stations will promote the film. The press kit should concentrate on stars, director, and the film's special elements.

Black-and-White Stills

Black-and-white stills are important for newspaper promotion. If the star has been contracted to go on a "junket,"* stills will be published in markets where the star's personal appearances take place.

Color Slides

A selection of eight to twelve slides should suffice.

Screening Cassettes

About 50 to 100 VHS screening cassettes should be submitted to exhibitors, TV stations, and magazines. Each cassette, needless to say, must be marked with the "for preview only" warning.

Electronic Press Kit

Behind-the-scenes footage should be assembled with the star's interviews, short film scenes, and other interesting segments, and submitted to the entertainment division of local news shows.

Release Plan

In no way can a small, low-budget film compete with major studio releases. The major distributors control and own the most lucrative theater chains, and understandably favor major releases. It is difficult to get into any of these chains, but every effort should be made to get the film at least in a few lucrative theaters.

Initial (test) Release

These initial tests should be conducted prior to June, as by the end of June the majors have scheduled their summer releases. These tests should be conducted at three or four screens in smaller cities, such as Fresno, California, Las Vegas, Nevada, Phoenix, Arizona, and Madison, Wisconsin. At this time the ad campaign *must* be completed, as exhibitors want to see the campaign before they commit their theaters.

---

*A personal appearance tour is unusual for a small, low-budget film.

The first test has to prove that the box office (based on publicity and advertising campaigns) generated sufficient three-day-per-screen averages, followed by somewhat less, but still acceptable, seven-day averages. The second test (the film is shown in three or four theaters in a different area) should verify the result of the first test.

Primary Release

The primary release should take place in early fall, when few major studio films are released. The film should stay on screens until Thanksgiving to give it a favorable home video exposure.

Successful performance:

The film should play for two to four weeks on multiple screens in first-rate theaters.

Moderate performance:

The film plays in lesser theaters at a reduced rental rate for about two-week runs in several areas.

Poor performance:

The film will be paired with another film, and will run as second feature.

EXHIBIT A

PERFORMER'S COPY

STANDARD AFTRA (EXCLUDING EXTRAS) EMPLOYMENT CONTRACT

Date _____ , 19 ____

Between _____ , Producer, and

_____ , Performer. Producer engages
Performer and Performer agrees to perform services for Producer in television commercials as follows:

Commercial Title(s) and Code No(s) _____ No. of Commercials _____

Check if Applicable
- ☐ Dealer Commercial(s)
  - ☐ Type A
  - ☐ Type B
- ☐ Seasonal Commercial(s)
- ☐ Test or Test Market Commercial(s)
- ☐ Non-Air Commercial(s)
- ☐ Produced for Cable

Such commercial(s) are to be produced by _____

Advertising Agency _____ Address _____

acting as agent for _____

Advertiser _____ Product(s) _____

City and State in which services rendered: _____ Place of Engagement: _____

( ) Principal Performer	( ) Solo or duo	( ) Signature - solo or duo
( ) Stunt Performer	( ) Group-3-5	( ) Group-Signature-3-5
( ) Puppeteer	( ) Group-6-8	( ) Group-Signature-6-8
( ) Specialty Act	( ) Group-9 or more	( ) Group-Signature-9 or more
( ) Dancer	( ) Contractor	( ) Pilot
( ) Singer		

Classification: On Camera _____ Off Camera _____ Part to be Played _____

Compensation: _____ Date & Hr. of Engagement: _____

Check if: Flight Insurance ($10) Payable ☐
Wardrobe to be furnished by Producer ☐ by Performer ☐

If furnished by Performer, No. of Costumes @ $12.50 _____ @ $20.00 _____ Total Wardrobe Fee $ _____
(Non-Evening Wear) (Evening Wear)

☐ Performer does not consent to the use of his/her services in commercials made hereunder as dealer commercials payable at dealer commercial rates.
☐ Performer does not consent to the use of his/her services in commercials made hereunder on a simulcast.

The standard provisions printed on the reverse side hereof are a part of this contract. If this contract provides for compensation at AFTRA minimum, no addition, changes or alterations may be made in this form other than those which are more favorable to the Performer than herein provided. If this contract provides for compensation above AFTRA minimum, additions may be agreed to between Producer and Performer which do not conflict with the provisions of the AFTRA Television Recorded Commercials Contract, provided that such additional provisions are separately set forth under "Special Provisions" hereof and signed by the Performer.

Performer authorizes Producer to make all payments to which Performer may be entitled hereunder by check payable to Performer and sent to the AFTRA office nearest the city in which the commercial was made.

All notices to Producer shall be addressed as follows:

To Producer at _____

This contract is subject to all of the terms and conditions of the AFTRA Television Recorded Commercials Contract. Employer of Record for income tax and unemployment insurance purposes is _____

PRODUCER (NAME OF COMPANY) _____

BY _____ PERFORMER _____

Performer hereby certifies that he or she is 21 years of age or over. (If under 21 years of age this contract must be signed below by a parent or guardian.)

I, the undersigned hereby state that I am the _____ of the above named Performer and do hereby consent and give my permission to this agreement.   (Mother, Father, Guardian)

(Signature of Parent or Guardian)

SPECIAL PROVISIONS (including adjustments, if any, for Stunt Performers):

Performer acknowledges that he or she has read all the terms and conditions in the Special Provisions section above and hereby agrees thereto.

Performer _____ Social Security Number _____

IMPORTANT PROVISIONS ON BACK. PLEASE READ CAREFULLY.

(W-4 Form is attached here.)

The Independent Film and Videomaker Program

OVERVIEW

The Independent Film and Videomaker Program at The American Film Institute provides funding for animation, documentary, experimental and narrative projects. The purpose of this grant is to support experienced, professional independent media artists whose work shows exceptional promise and who have demonstrated a commitment to the art of the moving image. Irrespective of subject or genre, productions must emphasize creative use of the media, fulfilling and, when possible, extending the creative possibilities of film and video. The maximum grant award is $20,000. This program is highly competitive: approximately 3% of the applicants receive funding each year.

ELIGIBILITY

• Applications for non-commercial, non-instructional projects over which the applicant has overall control and primary creative responsibility and copyright are eligible.

• Applicants must be United States citizens or permanent residents (with Green Card) and must reside and work in the United States or its territories during the grant period.

• Grants will be awarded only to individual film and video artists. Artists who have previously received grants from the Independent Film and Videomaker program are not eligible to apply. ORGANIZATIONS ARE NOT ELIGIBLE TO APPLY.

• Applicants may not be enrolled as full-time students in an educational institution at the time of the application, three months prior to that time, or during the life of the grant. Projects associated with a degree program will not be funded.

• Applicants must submit only one project for consideration. Applications will be accepted for new projects and works in progress on 35mm, 16mm or professional video format only. Funding is not available for research or development of a project, distribution or subtitling. Grant monies are available for production and post-production only and may not be used for expenses incurred before the date of the grant contract.

• Grants will be awarded only to projects to be made within the United States. If principal photography has been completed in another country, the applicant may request finishing funds for projects to be completed in the United States.

• Employees of The American Film Institute, Fellows of the Center for Advanced Film and Television Studies, and individuals receiving grants or internships from the AFI are not eligible to apply until the conclusion of such affiliation.

CRITERIA

• Applications will be judged on the basis of creativity and originality of the proposed project and on the artistic merit and technical quality of the sample of previous work and proposed work in progress.

• Consideration will be given to the applicant's perceived ability to successfully complete the project as proposed and budgeted within the grant period of twenty-four months.

TO APPLY

1. Applicants must submit a copy of a completed work that originated on film (16mm or 35mm) or professional video format for which they have had significant creative responsibility. Applicants who have commenced production on their proposed project must submit a work in progress. It is to the applicant's advantage to send a previous work sample that is stylistically relevant to the proposed project. The sample of previous work and work in progress must be submitted on separate reels (16mm or 35mm) or cassettes (3/4" or VHS). *It is highly recommended that the applicant select a significant 10 minute segment of each sample, cued (video) or marked with paper (film).* Film/mag track or film/audio cassette will not be accepted. Both the container and reel or cassette must be prominently labeled with the applicant's name. *Please do not send original footage or master edits.* All films/tapes are returned via United Parcel Service (UPS) insured for $100.00. (UPS does not deliver to post office boxes; please provide street address.)

THE INDEPENDENT FILM AND VIDEOMAKER PROGRAM APPLICATION

(Please type)

NAME_____

ADDRESS_____

CITY_____ STATE_____ ZIP _____

PHONE - HOME (   )_____ BUSINESS (   )_____

U.S. CITIZEN YES_____ NO_____ PERMANENT RESIDENT YES____ NO_____ GREEN CARD # _____

PROPOSED PROJECT:	PREVIOUS WORK SAMPLE:
TITLE _____	TITLE _____
TOTAL BUDGET _____	TOTAL BUDGET _____
APPROXIMATE LENGTH _____	RUNNING TIME _____
ROLE OF APPLICANT _____	ROLE OF APPLICANT _____

GENRE OF PROPOSED PROJECT (check one only):
EXPERIMENTAL_____   DOCUMENTARY_____
ANIMATION_____   NARRATIVE_____

GENRE OF PREVIOUS WORK SAMPLE:
EXPERIMENTAL_____   DOCUMENTARY_____
ANIMATION_____   NARRATIVE_____

PROPOSED PROJECT TO BE COMPLETED IN:
35MM_____ 16MM_____ 1 INCH_____ 3/4 INCH____
COLOR_____ B/W_____ SOUND_____ SILENT____

ORIGINAL FORMAT OF PREVIOUS WORK:
35MM_____ 16MM_____ 1 INCH_____ 3/4 INCH____
COLOR_____ B/W_____ SOUND_____ SILENT____

FORMAT OF WORK-IN-PROGRESS SAMPLE:
35MM_____ 16MM_____ 3/4 INCH_____ VHS____
COLOR_____ B/W_____ SOUND_____ SILENT____
Running Time_____

FORMAT SUBMITTED WITH THIS APPLICATION:
35MM_____ 16MM_____ 3/4 INCH_____ VHS_____
COLOR_____ B/W_____ SOUND_____ SILENT____

BUDGET DESCRIPTION EXPENSES
(Fill in as applicable)

CONFIRMED INCOME AND CONTRIBUTIONS
(Documentation may be required)

1. Production staff	$_____	9. Personal Resources	_____
2. Talent	_____	10. Cash Donations	_____
3. Scripts, rights	_____	11. Other grants received	_____
4. Production expenses:		12. In-kind services	_____
Equipment rental	_____	13. Other	_____
Film and/or tape stock	_____	14. TOTAL CONFIRMED INCOME	_____
5. Travel, food, lodging	_____		
6. Post Production	_____	15. REMAINDER of total budget	
7. Other	_____	(line 8 minus line 14)	_____
8. TOTAL BUDGET	_____		

IFVP funds will be used for:
Production_____ Post-Production_____

AMOUNT REQUESTED
FOR THIS GRANT   _____

LIST **CONFIRMED** FUNDING SOURCES AND AMOUNTS

LIST **POTENTIAL** FUNDING SOURCES

SUMMARY OF PROPOSED PROJECT (Do not exceed space provided. Please include an accurate synopsis of content and a description of visual style if applicable.)

WHAT IS THE RELATIONSHIP BETWEEN THE SAMPLE SUBMITTED AND YOUR PROPOSED PROJECT? (Do not exceed space provided. Please discuss similarities in style and form as well as content.)

OTHER RELEVANT INFORMATION (Optional. Additional information you would like the panel to know about your work in general, your artistic development or what compels you to undertake this project at this time.)

SAMPLE

CHECKLIST FOR MAILING. **INCOMPLETE APPLICATIONS ARE NOT LIKELY TO BE FUNDED.**

❑ EIGHT IDENTICAL SETS OF APPLICATION
MATERIALS each including:
Application form
Resumes of principals
Itemized budget
Treatment for Animation, Documentary, or Experimental;
Script for Narrative

❑ Confirmation card with name, address and postage
❑ Return shipping label
❑ Completed IFVP File Card
❑ Identification on each container and each reel or tape
❑ Film or video sample of a completed work
❑ Work in progress if available
❑ A significant 10 minute segment marked on each sample work

I have read and understood the eligibility requirements presented herein and I certify that all of the foregoing statements are true and complete to the best of my knowledge. I certify that I am not currently enrolled as a full-time student in an educational institution, that I have not been enrolled in the previous three months; and that I would not be enrolled during the life of the IFVP grant. I acknowledge that The American Film Institute and The Independent Film and Videomaker Program are not liable for loss or damage to materials submitted.

Signature of Applicant_____Date_____

2. Applicants must submit **eight identical sets of application materials.** Each set should contain the following items **collated in the order listed:**

    A. Application form
    B. Current resumes of project principals, one to two pages each
    C. Itemized budget
    D. Brief treatment (for documentary, experimental and animation projects)
        or script (for narrative projects)

Each set of documents should be **assembled in exactly the order listed** and fastened with a staple in the upper left hand corner. Narrative scripts should be hole-punched on the left and fastened with two brass brads. Each set of narrative materials (documents A-D) should be secured with a rubber band. Please do not include extraneous cover sheets or plastic or paper covers.

In addition, applicants should enclose the following:

    E. Return shipping label
    F. Completed IFVP File Card
    G. Completed IFVP Confirmation Card

It is the responsibility of the applicant to ensure that all materials requested in the guidelines are provided in the format described. Improperly assembled materials will be returned.

Address package as listed below. To expedite handling please mark the abbreviation of the category to which you are applying in lower left corner of package or mail label: AN (Animation), DOC (Documentary), EX (Experimental), NARR (Narrative).

LIABILITY

The American Film Institute makes every effort to safeguard materials submitted for selection, but will not assume responsibility for loss or damage to work.

RIGHTS

Ownership and rights to the completed project will be retained by the film or video artist.

Grant recipients must agree to submit progress reports during the grant period. Upon completion of the work a final report and budget must be submitted with a copy of the completed work in its original format or two copies on 3/4" videocassette.

CALENDAR

Applications and support materials must be RECEIVED no later than 5:00 p.m. Tuesday SEPTEMBER 15, 1992. **Late applications will be rejected. Applications received after the closing date but postmarked on or before said date will not be accepted. In the interests of fairness to all applicants, there will be no exceptions.**

Announcements of awards will be made by APRIL 30, 1993.

Funding will be available after MAY 15, 1993.

MAIL MATERIALS TO:

The Independent Film and Videomaker Program
The American Film Institute
P.O. Box 27999
2021 N. Western Avenue
Los Angeles, CA 90027-1625

Mark package or mail label in lower left corner with category abbreviation: AN, DOC, EX, NARR.

FOR FURTHER INFORMATION CONTACT:

Grants Administrator
The Independent Film and Videomaker Program
(213) 856-7743

Bibliography

Alaraid, William. *Money Sources for Small Business*. Santa Maria, CA: Puma Publishing, 1991.

Blumenthal, Howard J. and Oliver R. Goodenough. *This Business of Television: A Practical Guide to the TV/Video Industries*. Billboard, 1991.

Chimerine, L., R. Cushman, and H. Ross, *Handbook for Raising Capital*. Homewood, IL: Dow Jones-Irwin, 1987.

Duda, Doug. *Guide to the Sponsorship Video*. White Plains, NY: Knowledge Industry Publications, 1987.

Houghton, Buck. *What a Producer Does*. Los Angeles: Silman-James, 1992.

Lipton, Lenny. *Independent Filmmaking*, rev ed. NY: Fireside, 1983.

Meyer, Richard T. *Survey of Seed Capital*. Atlanta: Emory Business School, 1991.

Motion Picture, TV and Theater Directory. Tarrytown, NY: Motion Picture Enterprises.

Penney, Edmund F. *The Facts on File Dictionary of Film and Broadcast Terms*. NY: Facts on File Publishers, 1991.

Schilit, W. Keith. *The Entrepreneur's Guide to Preparing a Winning Business Plan and Raising Venture Capital*. Englewood Cliffs, NJ: Prentice Hall, 1990.

Squire, Jason. *The Movie Business Book*, 2d ed. NY: Fireside, 1992.

Vogel, Harold L. *Entertainment Industry Economics*. NY: Cambridge University Press, 1990.

*I*ndex